Picasso in Chicago

*Paintings,
Drawings,
and Prints
from
Chicago
Collections*

*The Art Institute
of Chicago
February 3
March 31, 1968*

The Art Institute of Chicago

COVER: *No. 102. Study for the Chicago Sculpture. White chalk drawing on plywood. Gift of the Artist*

INSIDE FRONT AND BACK COVERS: *Chicago Civic Center Plaza, photographs by Ezra Stoller Associates, Inc. Reproduced by permission of the Public Building Commission of Chicago*

Subsequent to the age of princely patronage which can be said to have ended with the French Revolution, it has been given to few artists to achieve great fame and fortune during their lifetime. These achievements have not always gone together, but Pablo Picasso is surely a notable exception. At the age of eighty-six, he has gained an enviable reputation among artists, art historians, and critics, but he has also achieved popular acclaim given to few artists. On the occasion of his eighty-fifth birthday in 1966, the most comprehensive exhibition of his work ever assembled was seen in Paris by nearly 850,000 people, the largest number ever known to attend an art exhibition. Books, magazine articles, newspaper accounts, films, television programs about Picasso abound, and have made his name a household word. Why then another Picasso exhibition?

In few cities of the world has the work of Picasso been collected so extensively as in Chicago, and the Picasso collections of The Art Institute are among the richest of any general museum in the United States. Probably the first exhibition in Chicago of Picasso's work took place at The Arts Club in 1923, an exhibition of drawings selected by Picasso himself and containing a preface to the catalogue by the English critic Clive Bell. Subsequent exhibitions of Picasso's work were held at The Arts Club at fairly regular intervals, while examples of his work were shown at the Albert Roullier Galleries in the 'twenties and 'thirties and at the Chester Johnson Galleries in the 'twenties. Consequently Chicagoans may be said to have had wide exposure to the artist. By limiting this exhibition to Picasso in Chicago, it signalizes the homage that Chicagoans have paid to the greatest artist of our century.

During the summer of 1967, the city of Chicago dedicated in the Civic Center, the monumental sculpture which Picasso designed and donated to the city. This is the first opportunity that The Art Institute and through it the people of Chicago have had to honor the artist and express our gratitude to him for his notable generosity. The exhibition has been limited to paintings, drawings and prints owned by The Art Institute and by Chicago collectors. Two former Chicagoans, Mrs. Gilbert W. Chapman and Mrs. Wolfgang Schoenborn, have graciously consented to allow us to show important works which they acquired while living in Chicago. We are deeply indebted to the lenders for their great generosity in contributing to the exhibition and sharing in the homage we pay to Picasso.

Various members of the staff of The Art Institute have worked on assembling the exhibition, and the catalogue entries have been prepared in great part by Mrs. Judith di Meo for the paintings and Mrs. Marcelle Lukaszewski for the drawings and prints.

Surely this exhibition serves not only to show the richness of Chicago collections, but also the variety and depth of the production of the great artistic figure of our time, Pablo Picasso.

C. C. Cunningham, Director

Lenders to the Exhibition

Anonymous, 5, 30, 44, 47, 52, 53, 91
Mr. and Mrs. James W. Alsdorf, 18, 22, 48, 67, 84, 86, 92
The Alsdorf Foundation, 39, 45
The Arts Club of Chicago, 83
Mr. and Mrs. B. E. Bensinger, 21, 29
Mr. and Mrs. Edwin A. Bergman, 38
Mr. and Mrs. Leigh B. Block, 9, 27, 42
Mr. and Mrs. Michael Braude, 73
Mrs. Gilbert W. Chapman, 3, 17, 75, 80
Mr. and Mrs. Louis N. Cohen, 50
Mr. and Mrs. Nathan Cummings, 33, 36, 57
Mr. and Mrs. Roy Friedman, 15, 24
Mr. and Mrs. Willard Gidwitz, 43
William E. Hartmann, 104, 105
Mr. and Mrs. Edwin E. Hokin, 56, 69, 100
Mrs. Samuel E. Johnson, 103
Mr. and Mrs. Everett Kovler, 129, 131, 133, 135,
139, 144, 178
Roger McCormick, 6
Mr. and Mrs. Lewis Manilow, 176
Mr. and Mrs. Henry Markus, 55, 58
Mr. and Mrs. Morton G. Neumann, 14, 40, 74, 77, 81, 85,
93, 98, 99, 146, 162, 167, 171, 172, 174, 179, 180
Mr. and Mrs. Michael Newbury, 20, 41
Mr. and Mrs. Albert Newman, 46
The Heirs of Pauline Kohlsaat Palmer, 65, 88
Florene M. Schoenborn, 37, 95
Mr. and Mrs. Joseph R. Shapiro, 89, 94
Dr. Eugene Solow, 125, 127, 132, 134, 143
Dr. Paul Sternberg Trusts, 97
Mrs. Ernest B. Zeisler, 13, 19, 28, 32
and the collections of The Art Institute of Chicago

Picasso the Painter

The City of Chicago unveiled the heroic sculpture by Pablo Picasso in the Plaza of its new Civic Center just five months ago. It is the great artist's first monumental metal sculpture on such a scale to be used in any metropolitan center. It is also the latest acquisition of a major work of art by Picasso to augment these rich resources of the master's painting and sculpture which have for many years been accumulating in the public and private collections of Chicago. The inauguration of the new civic sculpture suggests—demands—the appropriateness of a local tribute to the world's most distinguished living artist in his eighty-sixth year. Accordingly, the Art Institute has mounted the present exhibition selected from among the painting and graphic work available in the city.

Comprehensive Picasso exhibitions have taken place at accelerating intervals over continually expanding areas of the globe during the twentieth century. Among these, his important anniversaries—most recently his eighty-fifth—have been occasions for major displays of his work. Each of these is greeted freshly as a major artistic celebration. There is no parallel in our time to the continuous excitement and anticipation provoked by every presentation of his painting or sculpture, not least the extraordinary ceremony which greeted the formal completion and installation of the recent Chicago monument. That a contemporary American city should have commissioned this work is sufficiently unique; that it should be received so extravagantly —including the intense controversy—is equally striking. It is difficult to remember any recent public work of art which has caused equivalent excitement on the official and private level, though the violent reaction which has so consistently greeted Picasso's every new exhibition is in itself an impressive indication of the artist's power. A bad, mediocre or insignificant artist does not stimulate major opposition.

There is not one of us who has not spent his life under exposure to the magic influence of Picasso and his fabulous reputation, and happily, there are these who have succumbed to the influence, thus making the present exhibition possible. The exhibition is a tribute to their prescience and judgment as well as to the absolute quality of the Picasso material on view. This is not an integrated group of paintings submitted to the public for any reappraisal of the artist. It is a retrospective view of Picasso paintings as they were independently collected by individuals. There is a chronological order, because there are enough works amassed by Chicago collectors at different times to make this inevitable. On the other hand, the balance of different periods is unequal for the same reasons. The exhibition does not pretend a complete coverage of the styles and variations which constitute Picasso's virtuosity, but there is the absorbing aspect of concentration on particular periods which, if accidental to the extent that unrelated persons were involved in the acquisition, is of great interest in the results of their taste over the years. At the time when Chicagoans were building their splendid collections of the French 19th century and Impressionism, the young Picasso, a tyro under the influence of the school, was not neglected. His paintings just before and following 1900 were secured in examples of the finest quality. A number of these were purchased by Chicagoans as early as the First World War and are included in the permanent collection of the Art Institute. Particularly noteworthy is the unusual interest in the difficult period of Analytical Cubism which exhibits a special strength in local holdings. The splendid group of paintings which has been built over the years in this museum is included in the exhibition. From 1901 through 1959, Picasso is followed from Impressionism through his most recent, romantically exuberant expressionism. The Institute paintings can be considered almost in terms of an index to the works of the same periods from private sources which elaborate each theme. Generally,

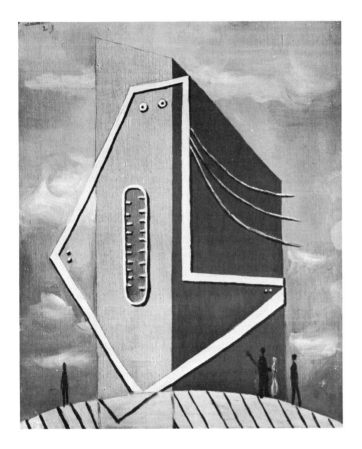

Picasso: Monument, Woman's Head, 1929
Private collection, France (not in exhibition)

the lacks are curiously consistent, as the strengths are note-worthy and unusual. The warm generosity of lenders is manifest in the composition of the exhibition, but it should not be overlooked that other commitments will unavoidably have resulted in the absence of many more exceptional paintings. Some aspects of Picasso's work have not been included here. The abundance of his ceramics in Chicago could constitute an entire exhibition. Most of the Picasso sculptures in the city have only recently been on view in the Art Institute in another, previous exhibition, and thus are not shown now.

The only three-dimensional work to be seen is the model for the Civic Center monument, and perhaps the present exhibition will help to clarify some of the problems which it has provoked. The subject has been a recurrent theme in Picasso's work since a painting of 1929, *Monument, Woman's Head* wherein the abstraction of the head is presented some fifty feet high with scale figures clustered at the base. This painting is unfortunately not owned in Chicago, but the same forms and idea have reappeared constantly in the artist's painting and sculpture, and there are five portraits in the exhibition which can help to elucidate the theme: *The Woman with the Flower* of 1932, *Portrait of Dora Maar,* 1939, *Seated Woman of* 1941, *Seated Woman* of 1949, and *Woman at the Mirror* of 1963. The last three of these paintings in particular show the same juxtaposition of the female features, the same nose treatment, emphasis on a single eye, and billowing hair, as in the monument. There is no question of Picasso's lifetime preoccupation with the female head as an object of universal physical beauty while he extends the image to encompass a symbolic and ethereal realm. It is surely no accident that in the experience of this sculpture the exquisite human characteristics become sublimated in a bird of peace. The aura of the monument spreads its wings, extends its shiny mane and inscrutable smile to follow the long course of its creator in the exhibition which honors him.

A. JAMES SPEYER
Curator of Twentieth Century Art

1   *Young Woman, 1900.*
The Art Institute of Chicago,
Gift of Joseph Winterbotham

3   *Peonies, 1901. Lent by Mrs. Gilbert W. Chapman*

2 *Nude with Cats, 1901. The Art Institute of Chicago, The Amy McCormick Memorial Collection*

4 *On the Upper Deck, 1901. The Art Institute of Chicago, Mr. and Mrs. Lewis L. Coburn Memorial Collection*

5　*Women and Child at the Fountain, 1901. Lent anonymously*

6 *Woman with Folded Arms, 1902. Lent by Roger McCormick*
7 *The Old Guitarist, 1903. The Art Institute of Chicago, Helen Birch Bartlett Memorial Collection*

8   *Woman with a Helmet of Hair, 1904.*
     The Art Institute of Chicago, Gift of Kate L. Brewster

9 *Nude with Pitcher, 1906. Lent by Mr. and Mrs. Leigh B. Block*

10   *Bust of Woman, 1906. The Art Institute of Chicago,*
      Gift of Florene May Schoenborn and Samuel A. Marx

11   *Seated Nude, 1909.*
The Art Institute of Chicago,
Gift of Florene May Schoenborn
and Samuel A. Marx

12   *Head of a Woman, 1909.*
The Art Institute of Chicago,
The Joseph Winterbotham Collection

13 *Woman Sewing, Paris, 1910.*
    Lent by Mrs. Ernest Zeisler

14 *Girl with Raised Left Arm, 1910.*
    Lent by Mr. and Mrs. Morton G. Neumann

15   *Woman with Mandolin, 1910. Lent by Mr. and Mrs. Roy Friedman*

16 *Daniel-Henry Kahnweiler, 1910. The Art Institute of Chicago,*
Gift of Mrs. Gilbert W. Chapman in memory of Charles B. Goodspeed

17   *Woman, 1910. Lent by Mrs. Gilbert W. Chapman*

19　*Glass, 1912. Lent by Mrs. Ernest Zeisler*

18　*Matches, Pipe, Glass, 1911.*
　　Collection of Mr. and Mrs. James W. Alsdorf

20 *"Au Bon Marché", 1912-1913.*
    Lent by Mr. and Mrs. Michael Newbury
21 *Bottle of "Marc de Bourgogne",*
    Glass, Newspaper, 1913.
    Lent by Mr. and Mrs. B. E. Bensinger

24   *Still Life, 1918.*
       Lent by Mr. and Mrs. Roy Friedman

22   *Glass, 1914.*
       Collection of Mr. and Mrs. James W. Alsdorf

23   *Man with a Pipe, 1915.*
       The Art Institute of Chicago.
       Gift of Mrs. Leigh B. Block
       in memory of Albert D. Lasker

25 *Mother and Child, 1921. The Art Institute of Chicago*

30   *Seated Woman, 1924. Lent anonymously*   29   *Bust of a Woman, 1923. Lent by Mr. and Mrs. B. E. Bensinger*

26   *Still Life, 1922. The Art Institute of Chicago, Ada Turnbull Hertle Fund*

27 *Still Life with Bread, Glass,*
   Camembert, Knife, 1922.
   Lent by Mr. and Mrs. Leigh B. Block
28 *Harlequin, 1923.*
   Lent by Mrs. Ernest Zeisler

31   *Head, 1927. The Art Institute of Chicago, Gift of Florene May Schoenborn and Samuel A. Marx*

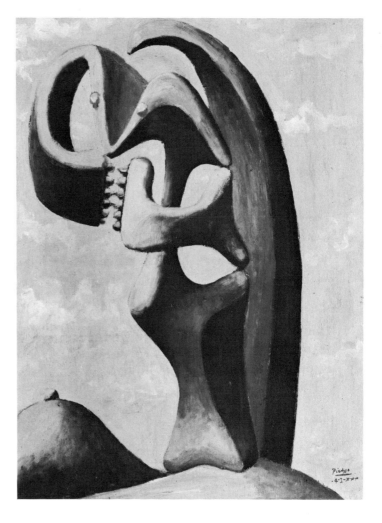

34 *Abstraction: Background with Blue Cloudy Sky, 1930*
    The Art Institute of Chicago, Gift of Florene May Schoenborn
    and Samuel A. Marx, and the Wilson L. Mead Fund

32 *Head, 1928. Lent by Mrs. Ernest Zeisler*

33

35   *The Red Armchair, 1931. The Art Institute of Chicago, Gift of Mr. and Mrs. Daniel Saidenberg*
33   *Woman, Sculpture and Vase of Flowers, 1929. Lent by Mr. and Mrs. Nathan Cummings*

36 *Woman with a Flower, 1932. Lent by Mr. and Mrs. Nathan Cummings*

37   *Girl Writing, 1934. Lent by Florene M. Schoenborn*

38   *Portrait of Dora Maar, 1939. Lent by Mr. and Mrs. Edwin A. Bergman*

40 *Seated Woman, 1941. Lent by Mr. and Mrs. Morton G. Neumann*

39 *Head of a Woman, 1940.*
    Lent by the Alsdorf Foundation

41 *Still Life with Basket of Cherries, 1943.*
    Lent by Mr. and Mrs. Michael Newbury

42   *Chair with Gladiolas, 1943. Lent by Mr. and Mrs. Leigh B. Block*

43 *Woman with Cat, 1944. Lent by Mr. and Mrs. Willard Gidwitz*

47 *Head of a Woman, 1949.*
  Lent anonymously

44 *The Vase of Flowers, 1947-1948.*
  Lent anonymously

46   *Seated Woman, 1949. Lent by Mr. and Mrs. Albert Newman*

45 *Still Life with Pitcher*
and Candlestick, 1945-46.
Lent by
the Alsdorf Foundation

48 *Villa and Palm Tree, 1951.*
Collection of
Mr. and Mrs. James W. Alsdorf

49   *The Reader, 1953. The Art Institute of Chicago,*
Gift of Mr. and Mrs. Arnold H. Maremont through the Kate Maremont Foundation

50 *Woman with Scarf, 1953. Lent by Mr. and Mrs. Louis N. Cohen*

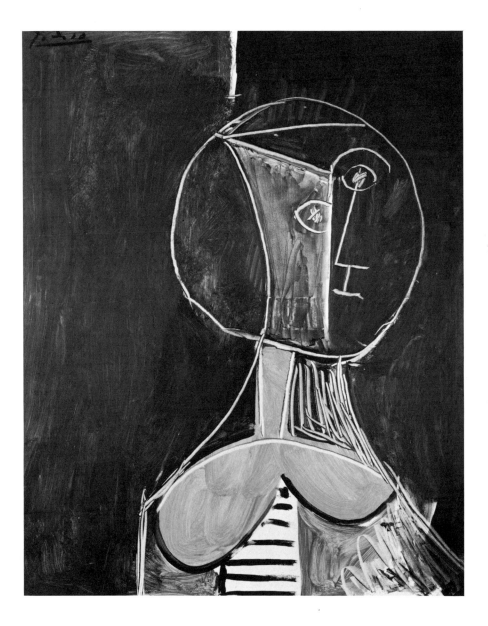

51 *Sylvette, 1954. The Art Institute of Chicago, Gift of Mr. and Mrs. Leigh B. Block*
52 *Bust of a Woman in Colors, 1956. Lent anonymously*

54   *Nude Under a Pine Tree, 1959. The Art Institute of Chicago, Grant J. Pick Collection*

53 *Bullfight, 1956. Lent anonymously*
55 *Woman by the Side of a Stream, 1960.*
    Lent by Mr. and Mrs. Henry Markus

56   *Bust of Woman with Hat, 1962. Lent by Mr. and Mrs. Edwin E. Hokin*

57 *Woman with Dog, 1962. Lent by Mr. and Mrs. Nathan Cummings*

58 *Woman with Mirror, 1963. Lent by Mr. and Mrs. Henry Markus*

Picasso the Draughtsman

Picasso's draughtsmanship has been one of the most engrossing phenomena of modern art for nearly seventy years, and remains for many both a constant thread leading through the labyrinth of his artistic development and a crucible of the artist's inventiveness, wherein one may see, as it were, his molten ideas taking form. The very beginnings of the exercise of Picasso's artistic vocation occur at a time, still in his adolescence, when the tradition and practice of academic drawing was yet the dominant technique for the discipline and refinement of talent. The very early charcoal and conté crayon studies of casts from the antique, the nude, and so forth which survive demonstrate that in his teens, Picasso, thanks to the advantages of being reared in an artistic household and to his vigorous innate gift, had considerable mastery of the classic form-study which this approach to drawing is intended to instill. Along with these school pieces and training works there are ebullient squibs and sketches, reflecting both a high-spirited playfulness and capacity for deep sympathetic feeling in the artist's nature.

In the Barcelona of the 'nineties and turn-of-the-century Paris Picasso kept, in the fashion of Steinlen and Toulouse-Lautrec, sketchbooks full of scenes of café life, thumbnail portraits, and other such informal subjects. The little page titled *At the Cabaret* of about 1900 belonging to the Art Institute is an energetic and sharply observed example of the genre. In its small format, it contains an authoritative feeling for compositional handling and rapid characterization which remain as hallmarks of Picasso's style.

The artist's familiarity with academy procedures in drawing, particularly the notion of utilizing drawing as a tool preparatory to painting, ensured that during his first artistic maturity, the Blue Period of 1901-1904, Picasso both continued to draw from life, particularly from the model, and also to use a more free and informal kind of drawing to set down figures and compositional ideas which were intended to come to full realization in paintings. By 1906, when Picasso had undertaken a number of very large and ambitious compositions in an attempt to set down monumental statements of his now securely realized artistic identity, there is a corresponding increase in the size and scale of the drawings, whether they are autonomous works such as the splendid *Portrait of Fernande Olivier,* or plans and preparations for paintings, such as the *Peasant Girls from Andorra* and the impressive *Two Nudes,* one of the studies for the great proto-Cubist painting now in the collection of The Museum of Modern Art.

During the Cubist period, drawing assumes a role even more crucial to the development of Picasso's painting. Such impressive works as the *Man with Crossed Hands* of 1907 in the Alsdorf Collection lay out compositional ideas with boldness and audacity and reveal in their powerful sweep the impatient artist's hand and his excitement at the simultaneous discovery and creation of a new language of form. The Analytical Cubist heads of 1909 demonstrate that concern with volumetric structure and architectonic composition which distinguish Picasso's work at this time are given the fullest treatment in such drawings, resulting in exceptional works. The grandeur and force of the greatest of these, such as the Art Institute's great *Head of a Woman,* do not take second place to the paintings of the same epoch. The atmospheric ambivalences of Cubist painting in 1911-1912 have their direct analogues in the richness and shimmer of the charcoal drawings of the period; the immediately subsequent cross-fertilization between drawing and collage is marked in the grand and severe *Still Life with Bottle* in the collection of Mr. and Mrs. Morton G. Neumann. The development of Cubism in these critical years is admirably laid out in the sequence of the pen and watercolor *Still Life* of 1907-1908 in the Art Institute collection, the lovely and sophisticated lyricism of the pen and ink *Still Life* of 1911 belonging to Mr. and Mrs. Michael Braude, and the classic charcoal and collage in the Neumann collection, of 1912-1913.

The high decorative phase of Synthetic Cubism, at nearly full tide by 1916, was yet another period in which Picasso uses drawing media to probe deeply into questions at the heart of his painting. The Art Institute's little gouache and watercolor, the *Woman in an Armchair* of that year, is an excellent demonstration of the artist's concern for exploring the question of monumental scale in an essentially two dimensional decorative kind of form, and in a small, even tiny, format. It is easy, however, to see how such a solidly constructed composition would easily lend itself to transposition to a very large scale without any loss of concentration or intensity. The number and variety of these small works suggest that Picasso enjoyed the paradox of creating truly grand compositions that might be easily held in the hand. This somewhat northern proclivity appears again later, in 1930, when Picasso made a number of free and fantastic variations on the Crucifixion panel of Grünewald's Isenheim Altarpiece. This desire to explore the possibilities of epic compositions in intimate formats runs through the remarkable Ingres-like portrait drawings of 1915 and 1916 as well, and continues into 1920 in the important series of silverpoint drawings with the subject of Nessus and Dejanira.

These unusual drawings pursue a specific artistic end within the double limitations of a restricted format and the employment of an especially difficult medium. The technique is directly analogous to drypoint in the way that it hardly admits of correction or alteration, and so the artist must put down his thought authoritatively and without hesitation. The spirited Nessus and Dejanira drawing in the collection of Mr. and Mrs. Morton G. Neumann is early in the series, dated September 14, 1920 and both pentimenti and second thoughts visible in it show that Picasso is here in the act of refining the idea from a number of variant possibilities. This glimpse into the artist's working procedures is made the more fascinating by the audacious free handling he uses. The Art Institute owns another drawing of the subject, dated September 22, 1920, a week later, where the entire conception of the work has been crystallized. The line, loose and agitated in the Neumann drawing, is now relentless in its purity and incisiveness and the protagonists of the dramatic subject stand eternally in the critical moment of the action.

The subject of Nessus and Dejanira, belonging to the heroic cycle of the Hercules legends, is important in Picasso's art because it is the initial appearance of the half-human half-animal creatures of classical legend which figure so prominently in his subsequent production. The centaur Nessus' abduction of Dejanira ends in his death (Hercules' powerful bow brings him down), but before dying he treacherously tells Dejanira that his blood is a love philtre when in fact it is a corrosive poison.

Later, her unknowing use of this poison results in Hercules' death. The subject then is full of overt and implied emotions of very high voltage—desire, love, death, betrayal and vengeance. A decade and more later these currents receive more explicit exfoliation in the etchings for Ovid's *Metamorphoses* and the subsequent hundred plates of the Vollard suite.

During the 'twenties the classical subjects introduced at the beginning of the decade come to portray a world of sober poetry, inhabited by pipers, dancers, and white-draped women whose repose is tinged with melancholy. The great paintings of this epoch, to which many of the drawings of the time are closely related, have a colossal grandeur of static form like that of late antique sculpture. The grandiose *Classical Head* in colored chalks belonging to the Arts Club of Chicago, together with the large *Mother and Child* oil of 1922 in the Art Institute are perfectly realized statements of the calm and ponderous dignity pervading Picasso's work in these halcyon years. The sculptural force of this approach to form remains prominent in the 'thirties, when it comes to be animated with vigorous movement, grand gesture, and baroque composition. The epitome of this impassioned style is the powerful *Minotaur and Woman* of 1933 recently acquired by the Art Institute. The subject of this drawing is one of the main themes of Picasso's art during the 'thirties and throughout a series of prints for the Vollard suite and in three outsize etchings executed in 1934-1935 the saga of the Minotaur is given in epic fashion. The artist uses the fabulous hybrid as his hero and personal symbol in a variety of situations charged with metaphysical import. In prints and related drawings the Minotaur stands for the search for wholeness of mind and being that is the essence of transcendental love. In the *Minotaur and Woman* drawing it is clear that the Minotaur speaks for the artist in his awareness that the metaphysical love just mentioned may be expressed by the image of desire blended with empathetic awareness. The Minotaur's action and gaze reveal a virile tenderness and faithful regard, while the woman he embraces is arched backwards in a fainting rapture. Her expression is vacant and her eyes blank; the awareness she betrays in the sketchy foot which barely presses against the Minotaur's side is far below the level of conscious thought and is purely involuntary. The medium and materials used in this work are exceptional in the way in which they amplify the mood and feeling of the image per se. The brisk and swelling pen strokes over sumptuous washes of *encre de chine* perfectly articulate the urgent gesture of the Minotaur and the beautiful blue paper of the drawing sets a wonderfully apt nocturnal mood, as if the whole were a vision of the night materialized under moonlight. The placement of the composition on the page is surpassing evidence of Picasso's attention to the suitability of format, and is the refinement of a unified vision toward which related works in other media, particularly prints, had moved. A particularly exhilarating aspect of this expert mise en page is the way in which contours of the various forms graze the edge of the paper now and again, enhancing the sense of barely contained energies in the coils and thrusts of the figures themselves. This imagistic concentration has the excitement both of surpassing virtuosity and an explosive impact.

The climactic point reached in Picasso's art with the painting of the great mural Guernica in 1937 and the extraordinary series of preparatory drawings for it (most of which are small-ish), set the artist on the path of a new stylistic development which reaches from the late spring of 1937 through 1945. During 1938 a number of curious and memorable pen and ink drawings of women, usually seated in a wicker chair, show the first post-Guernica phases of this new style which in its subject matter centers on the likeness of Picasso's new companion, Dora Maar. Emphatic striations derived from the wicker are used within the figures themselves, the whole forming groups of ladderlike designs which are almost painfully lively as they torque and shear through the compositions. The vigorous drawing in the collection of Mr. and Mrs. Morton G. Neumann is a prime example of the type.

During the 'forties, Picasso's draughtsmanship parallels the grave intensity of his wartime paintings, and comes, by 1945, to engage seriously with a number of ideas for large compositions. Often the same idea may be given form in various media and with different degrees of resolution; as the Art Institute's finely worked pencil drawing *Woman Bathing Her Foot* of 1944 has a counterpart in brush and wash in the collection of the Museum of Modern Art. This ink and wash technique is used in a wonderful luminous drawing, *Head of a Young Boy* belonging to Florene M. Schoenborn. Dated 1944, this drawing tells of the melancholy acceptance of life by youth which has known little but long years of war. The fragile innocence of the child harks back to similar qualities in the youthful saltimbanques of the Blue period.

The wonderful series of the artist and model in the studio certainly dominated Picasso's drawings from the 1950's. These rich drawings, almost invariably in black ink applied with the brush, are distinguished by their startling virtuosity and, perhaps more interestingly, for the lightly mocking and satirical tome with which they are invested. In them we may see the wizened artist, peering at his work in the easel before him, so absorbed in his art that he is ludicrously oblivious to the blooming femininity of his voluptuous models. In other drawings bizarre groups of studio visitors, amateurs, critics, dealers, collectors, students and scruffy young artists wander aimlessly about the studio or gaze abstractedly at the works stacked about the walls. These subjects are an unusual indication of the artist's own awareness of the extraordinary temporal range of his activities, and so they mark in a way, a conscious entrance upon a *Spatstil,* an artistic viewpoint which for Picasso has a rather retrospective character. The tart humor of these works is not directed to the outside world alone; certainly the artist aims most of the barbs at himself, and can see with rueful good nature that the pungency of old age will very likely go unnoticed by youth in its freshness or by the pompous self-importance of middle maturity. In recent years Picasso has continued to draw with his customary virtuosity and vigor, and has often returned to themes and subjects which have especially engaged his attention in the past. Clowns and youthful models, pastoral figures of pipers and shepherds, animals, children, and the whole range of personages from the corrida and the studio may be mixed together in agreeable scenes radiant with the sense of well-being and joy of life which mark the artist's autumnal years.

DENNIS ADRIAN

Assistant Curator of Prints and Drawings

59   *At the Cabaret, ca. 1898-1900. The Lewis L. Coburn Memorial Collection*
60   *Two Figure Studies, 1904. Gift of Robert Allerton*

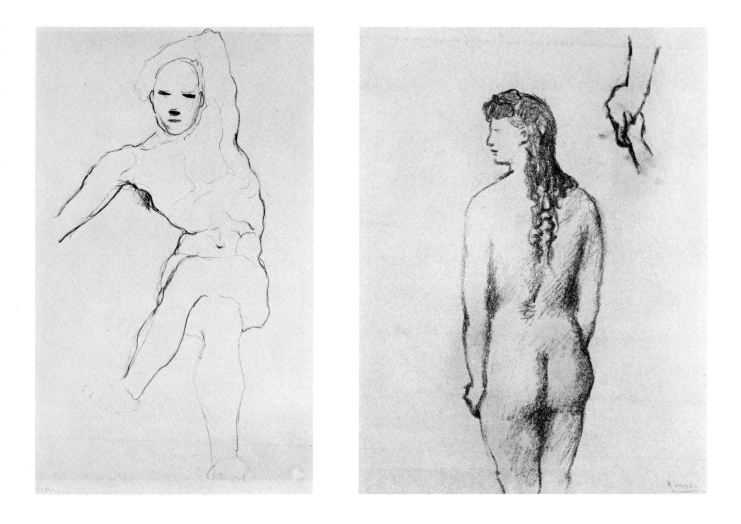

61   *Study of a Seated Man, ca. 1905.*
      Gift of Robert Allerton

62   *Female Nude Seen from the Back, ca. 1906.*
      Gift of Walter S. Brewster

63   *Portrait of Fernande Olivier, 1906. Gift of Herman Waldeck*

64   *Peasant Girls from Andorra, 1906.*
     Gift of Robert Allerton

65   *Peasant Woman with a Shawl, 1906.*
     Lent by the Heirs of Pauline Kohlsaat Palmer

66   *Two Nudes, 1906. Gift of Mrs. Potter Palmer*

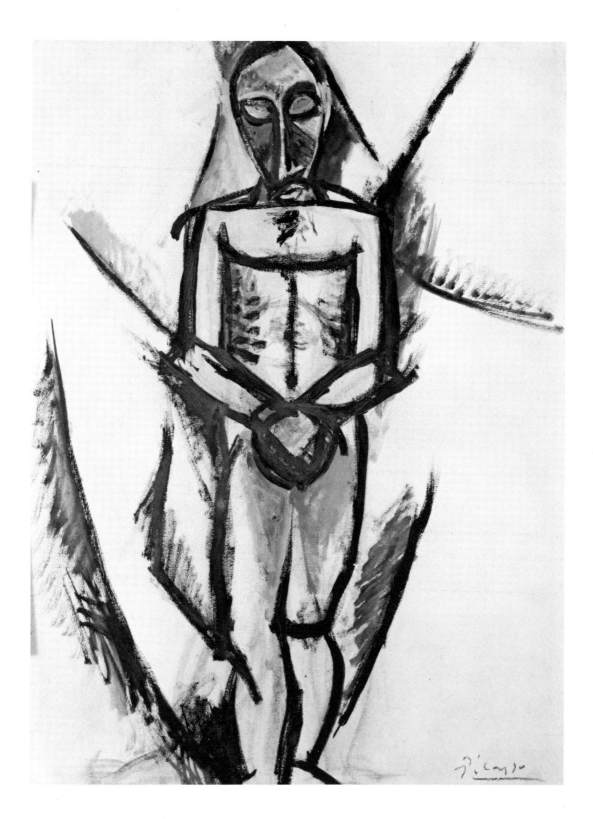

67 *Man with Crossed Hands, 1907. Lent from the Collection of Mr. and Mrs. James W. Alsdorf*

68 *Still Life, 1907-08.*
   Gift of William Eisendrath, Jr.

69 *Head of a Woman, 1908.*
   Lent by Mr. and Mrs. Edwin E. Hokin

70   *Head of a Woman, 1909. The Charles L. Hutchinson Memorial*

71 *Head, 1909.*
The Alfred Stieglitz Collection

72 *Head of a Woman, 1909.*
Gift of Mr. and Mrs. Roy J. Friedman

74   *Still Life with a Bottle, 1912-13. Lent by Mr. and Mrs. Morton G. Neumann*

73 *Still Life, 1911. Lent by Mr. and Mrs. Michael Braude*
75 *Still Life with Calling Card, 1914. Lent by Mrs. Gilbert W. Chapman*

76   *Woman in an Armchair, 1916. Gift of Robert Allerton*

78   *Portrait of Massine, 1917.*
Gift of Mrs. Gilbert W. Chapman
in memory of Charles B. Goodspeed

77　*Costume Design for Pulcinella, 1917. Lent by Mr. and Mrs. Morton G. Neumann*

79   *Pierrot and Harlequin, 1918. Gift of Mrs. Gilbert W. Chapman in memory of Charles B. Goodspeed*

80   *Pierrot and Harlequin, 1919. Lent by Mrs. Gilbert W. Chapman*

81   *Nessus and Dejanira, 1920. Lent by Mr. and Mrs. Morton G. Neumann*

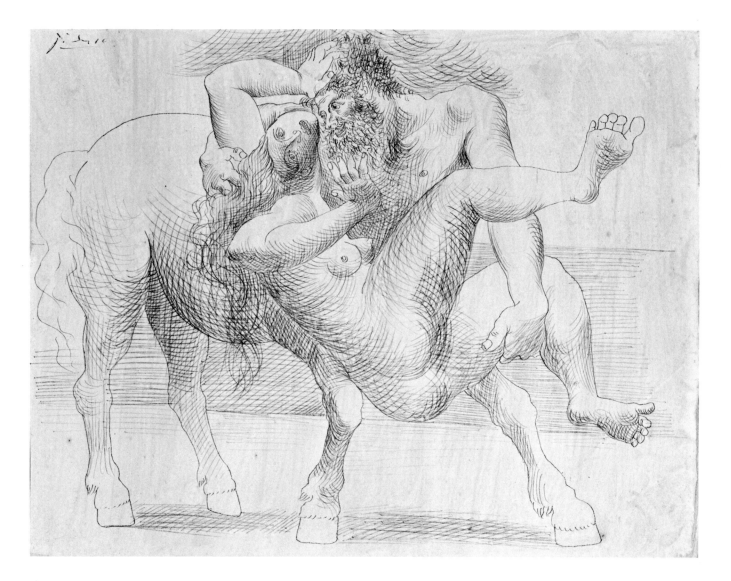

82   *Nessus and Dejanira, 1920. The Clarence Buckingham Collection*

83   *Classical Head, ca. 1921. Lent by The Arts Club of Chicago*

84 *Young Girl Seated, 1921.*
    Lent from the Collection of
    Mr. and Mrs. James W. Alsdorf

85 *Sheet of Figure Studies, ca. 1921-23.*
    Lent by Mr. and Mrs. Morton G. Neumann

86   Nude, 1923.
     Lent from the Collection of Mr. and Mrs. James W. Alsdorf

88   *Two Dancers, 1925.*
     Lent by the Heirs of Pauline Kohlsaat Palmer

87   *The Pipes of Pan, 1923. Bequest of Joseph Winterbotham*

91   *Minotaur and Wounded Horse, 1935. Lent anonymously*

89 The Flute Player, 1932.
    Lent by
    Mr. and Mrs. Joseph R. Shapiro

92 Portrait of Dora Maar, 1936.
    Lent from the Collection of
    Mr. and Mrs. James W. Alsdorf

93   *Woman Seated in a Wicker Chair*
     (Dora Maar), 1938. Lent by
     Mr. and Mrs. Morton G. Neumann

94   *Seated Woman, 1941.*
     Lent by Mr. and Mrs. Joseph R. Shapiro

95 *Head of a Young Boy, 1944. Lent by Florene M. Schoenborn*

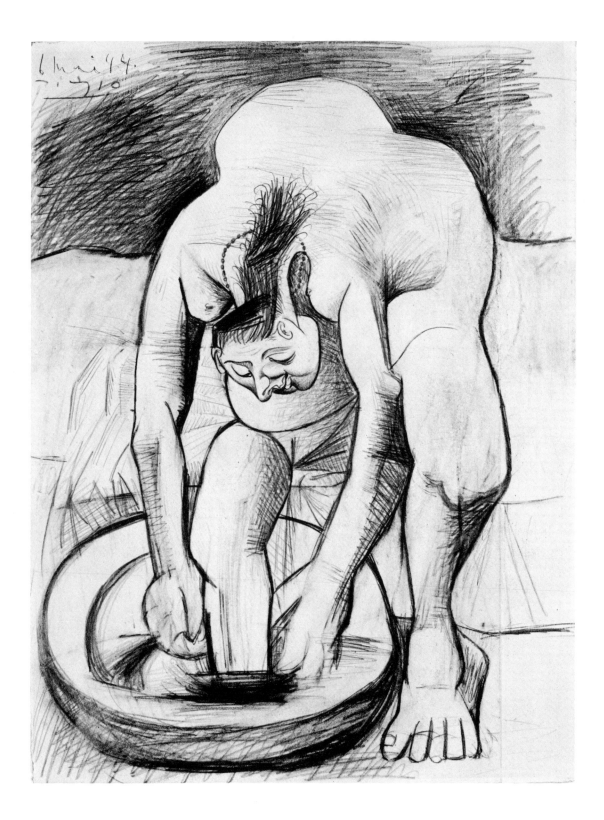

96   *Woman Bathing Her Foot, 1944. Bequest of Curt Valentin*

97   *Seated Woman, 1953. Lent by Dr. Paul Sternberg Trusts*

99   In the Studio, 1954. Lent by Mr. and Mrs. Morton G. Neumann

98   *Studio Scene, 1953. Lent by Mr. and Mrs. Morton G. Neumann*

100   *The Reading, 1953.*
       Lent by
       Mr. and Mrs. Edwin E. Hokin

103   *Reclining Woman, 1964. Lent by Mrs. Samuel E. Johnson*

104   *Study for the Chicago Sculpture, 1965.*
Lent by William E. Hartmann

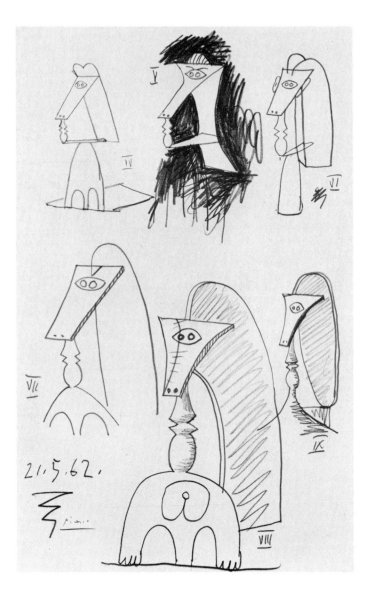

101 *Sheet with Six Studies for the Chicago Sculpture, 1962.*
Gift of William E. Hartmann

105 *Head, 1965. Lent by William E. Hartmann*

106   Man and Flute Player, 1967. Bequest of Loula Lasker

Picasso the Printmaker

Along with a few other twentieth century masters, Picasso fully merits the epithet of *peintre-graveur,* or artist-printmaker, bestowed upon him by the first cataloguer of his prints, Bernard Geiser. The term denotes something more than the occasional practice of making prints by an artist who is a painter. It is reserved for those artists whose printmaking is at the very core of their creative concerns, along with works in other media, particularly the obviously related activities of painting and drawing. With Picasso, it is a truism that his prints have been a major part of his *oeuvre* for more than sixty years, but it is a less familiar fact that in several periods of great moment in the artist's career, printmaking is his central vehicle of expression, and the chief works of these fascinating times are extraordinary masterpieces. It is particularly gratifying to be able to note that Chicago collections, both public and private, contain most of these extremely important prints in examples of the highest quality. Artistically precocious and coming to early adulthood in the 'nineties, when the sophistication of modern printmaking reached a high-water mark throughout Europe, Picasso inevitably tried his hand at a plate or two. His first print, *El Zurdo,* done in Barcelona in 1899, is a piece of juvenilia, combining a period satirical flavor with a technique loosely modelled on Goya's *Caprichos.* After this modest start, Picasso does not turn again to printmaking until he is finally, if precariously, settled in Paris. The several years of flirtation with the styles of the 'nineties, the vigorous elegance of Lautrec, pointillism, and the feeling of Parisian life of the time are put aside by the emergence of the haunting and idiosyncratic visions of the Blue Period. In this first artistic maturity, Picasso again turns to printmaking, and with a basic knowledge of intaglio techniques provided by his friend, Ricardo Canals, tackles a large zinc plate to produce the best-known of all his prints, the great etching, *The Frugal Repast.* This astonishing print epitomizes the themes of the Blue Period—the artist's concern with blindness, poverty, hunger, and the senses (particularly touch), and is a poetic distillation of the harsh realities of daily existence. The Art Institute is particularly fortunate to have in its collection not only the brilliant and rich impression of this print taken before the steel facing of the plate, which comes from the Stieglitz Collection, but a superb and unique early impression in blue ink as well. These impressions, through the richness of the still fresh plate and the sensitivity of the inking, are paragons of quality. Subsequent prints of this period explore the possibilities of drypoint, that difficult and demanding medium which requires the utmost in draughtsmanly marksmanship from the artist and permits no errors. The tender plates of acrobats and circus subjects done in 1905 contain a sensitive control of the drypoint needle

that is rhythmically expressive and sublimely economical in its descriptive function. During this early period Picasso experimented somewhat with woodcut, emulating the direct and powerful handling that Gauguin had introduced. Most of these prints are rather small, and exist in only a few proofs, but the largest of them, the imposing *Bust of a Girl,* 1906, was pulled in small edition in 1933.

During the development of Cubism, the discipline of a new language of form was brought to the challenges implicit in intaglio prints, and the artist produced a variety of ambitious compositions in all sizes. The lyrical approach to classical order in the watershed year of 1912 receives its most expressive statement in the large etching *Still Life with a Bottle,* known also as *Vie Marc* after the legend on the brandy bottle label in the composition.

The 'twenties see Picasso beginning to familiarize himself with the only print medium he had not hitherto approached, lithography. By 1930 his command of the technique begins to reveal the special qualities and possibilities of the medium, and there are advances over the rather informal efforts of a decade earlier. Properly, however, the decade of the 'twenties is consecrated to the ultimate refinement of Picasso's linear style in several groups of wonderful etchings, principally the plates for Balzac's curious *Le Chef d'Oeuvre Inconnu,* and the larger group for Ovid's *Metamorphoses.* The world of classical antiquity, with its immense range of subjects covering all manner of human feeling and action, yet presented within the many levels of meaning attaching to the forms of myth and allegory, attracted the artist with the possibility of using these themes as vehicles for a very personal, even autobiographical, expression. As the clowns and acrobats of the blue and rose periods provided Picasso with a cast of personages through which private emotional concerns were stated, the artist and model groups of the Balzac plates and the full pantheon available through Ovid's poem enlarged the scope of the mythical and semi-private allegorical themes.

The pure line which distinguished the drypoints of 1904-1906 reappears more suave and lyrical than before in the classical etchings, bringing to life an immutable arcadian world redolent with nostalgia. The sources of this remarkable Apollonian style of Picasso's carry with them a metaphysical overtone that is subsumed in the runs of invention Picasso presents. The expressiveness and fluidity of Etruscan mirror engraving, which Picasso knew and enjoyed greatly, brings to mind the fact that the polished etching plate is of course a kind of mirror wherein the artist may both see and present the truth: the reversal of image common to both mirrors and most kinds of printmaking is perhaps a parallel too cogent to be dismissed as an irrelevancy in the expanding of meanings and connections necessary to the full comprehension of Picasso's classical prints. Art as the mirror of inner life and feeling is another link in this chain of associations and in aggregate these associations may be said, with the Balzac series in 1927, to begin a decade of reflection and probing into the nature of artistic identity through art itself.

Le Chef d'Oeuvre Inconnu treats the relationship of painter and model in a fairly straightforward fashion, and within the framework of Balzac's story. In the subsequent Ovid plates the technique perfected for the Balzac series is given its head, and produces bursts of great brilliance, animated by the passion and breadth of the ancient poem.

The complete fulfillment of these currents in Picasso's graphic art, the probing of the artistic condition and the approach to the art and literature of the classical world as funds of images and forms with which to reveal private concerns of great intimacy, takes place within the hundred plates of the suite Vollard, executed between 1930 and 1937, and in the several great prints on the Minotauromachia theme etched in 1934 and 1935. The themes of the suite Vollard are numerous and complex. The warp of metaphysical import running through the whole is threaded with ideas and images appearing now in one context, now in another, changing meaning and inflection along the way, and being transformed into yet other forms and thoughts under the artist's burgeoning invention. The general sense of the group is that of a poetic reflection upon the artist's own life in its several modes. Rather than illustrating specific incidents in a reportorial way, Picasso forms images which articulate the psychic and emotional climate and events of inner reality.

The coupling figures of the so-called Battle of Love group reveal, in their churning rhythms and merging forms, the striving for unity of being which Plato called "the desire and pursuit of the whole." The form of love that Plato defines in this fashion is much more than merely physical: it is love as the force animating the drive to wholeness and completeness of being in thought and feeling of which physical love is but a symbol.

Where the Balzac plates of the late 'twenties dealt with the theme of the model and the painter, many plates of the suite Vollard are concerned with the artist as sculptor, in his studio, and with his models. In these scenes, the sculptor is usually seen as a figure of bearded maturity who regards his models and his works with an even-eyed calmness and authority. There is an Olympian repose in this series, as though the *artifex omnipotens* rested at the still point in the center of his creative world. Reclining with his model, the sculptor refreshes himself not with amorous dalliance, but with a benevolent survey of the elements of art and life. Nature is included in this lyrical mood, alluded to through vases of flowers and views of a peaceful landscape seen through a window.

The spell of this perfect and balanced world is disrupted in the parallel and contemporaneous group of prints that have as their protagonist the fabulous hybrid of man and bull, the Minotaur, who is the symbol of energy and animal force united with a human capacity for emotion. In Picasso's art, he is a pathetic and eventually tragic figure who is the complement to the dignified sculptor figure. The passion, high feelings, and life of the senses absent in the scenes of the Daedalean sculptor dominate the Minotaur's history. The flower-decked models of the Sculptor's Studio series attend the Minotaur in scenes of revelry. He possesses them lustily to the accompaniment of music and wine. Passion spent, he sleeps watched over by their calm and knowing gaze. The Minotaur's love is expressed in compositions which develop further the formal themes of the Battle of Love.

In the finest statements of this image, particularly the very great and masterful drawing in pen and wash on blue paper recently acquired by the Art Institute, the union symbolized, despite the Minotaur's partially animal nature, is not a mindless sensual coupling. The tender and loyally affectionate gaze of the creature speaks rather of the sympathetic pathos of the moment of love. The mood generated is that of desire tempered with awareness and empathy, the apotheosis of earthly love which, so transmuted, is ennobled to the level of an eternal principle.

Subsequently the story of the Minotaur takes two different courses: in one, the Minotaur meets death under the unblinking eyes of the models or Muses with whom he has disported. In the most powerful of these plates, dated May 26, 1933, the dying Minotaur assumes exactly the position he has in the ravishing large drawing on blue paper; the act of love as "a little death" is evoked. The alternative destiny granted by Picasso takes the form of another classic affliction, blindness. The blinded Minotaur, deprived of the all-important sense of sight, must be led about, dependent on the innocence and freshness of a little girl, carrying a dove or a bunch of flowers, who acts as his guide. This tragic situation in itself classic, echoing the fate of Oedipus at Colonnus. That the creature must rely on the sense of touch is the means with which Picasso resumes the current of the protagonist as a sculptor. The most haunting manifestation of the Blind Minotaur is the wonderful aquatint showing the agonized Minotaur reaching out pathetically to touch something while he is stared at by two fishermen and a sober pondering youth. The glow of the burnished plate appears to emanate from the radiant white dove carried by the accompanying little girl. The Minotaur seems both illuminated and consumed by this symbol of incandescent purity. His passions extinct, the Minotaur is led among those who wonder and muse on his fate.

It is in 1935 that Picasso produces the ultimate work dealing with the Minotaur, the *Minotauromachy*. This outsize plate, worked to great richness with both etching and drypoint, presents the Minotaur in a context more baffling than any previous one. At the edge of the sea, the Minotaur advances from the right toward a schoolgirl who holds a bouquet of flowers in one hand and a lighted candle aloft with the other. Between these two figures is a mortally wounded and panicked horse, across whose back is slung a woman in the costume of the bull ring. Her breasts bare, this remarkable figure rests her head, eyes closed, in the crook of one arm while with the other she points a torero's sword at the head of the stricken horse. To the left a bearded man clad in a loincloth ascends a ladder propped against a wall. From an adjacent building in the middle ground the entire extraordinary scene is watched by two girls at a window, upon whose sill rest dark and light doves. The meaning of this extremely important print requires us to move on to yet another level of understanding from the Minotaur plates of the suite Vollard; in those plates, the Minotaur speaks for the artist in most instances, if not as his *alter ego,* at least as a mouthpiece for individual concerns and experiences Picasso wishes to articulate. In the *Minotauromachy* the symbols and imagery retain the personal applications of the suite Vollard and in addition take on a larger metaphysical significance. The Minotaur appears here as a monster. His bestial aspects are emphasized with elaborate care. He is a dark power reaching out to extinguish or shield himself from the burning candle, which as it illuminates is consumed. The dying horse and the sleeping woman who are seen by this light are a vision of unthinking violence and physical agony. The bearded man, recalling the artist figures of the Balzac and Vollard suites, climbs the ladder to escape, but not without a mournful backward glance. The confrontations and oppositions symbolized variously by light and dark, the monstrous and the innocent, violence and the pacific (the doves), youth and age, and sunlight and shadow are the true subject of the *Minotauromachy*: the mingled natures of the Minotaur establish him as the ideal protagonist in an epic presentation of the mixed conflicts of these dualities. These themes of force and struggle, which delay the progress of the artist and are exposed by the light of innocent truth, both reflect difficulties in the artist's personal life and adumbrate the imminent storm of the Spanish Civil War. As a gathering together of threads of meaning and currents of feeling, the *Minotauromachy* remains among the most concentrated and momentous of all Picasso's productions.

That the artist felt the special import of the gathering tide of thought and emotion which led to the *Minotauromachy* is demonstrated by the unusual preparations of two huge etchings which anticipate it and work out aspects of the final imagery. One lays out the motif of the semi-nude woman in torero's garb, sprawled over the horse's back. The sensual face of an enormous bull confronts her nostril to nostril, and her eye widens in fear and amazement. In her outflung left arm she holds a sword, but she is powerless to use it. The horse she reclines upon is frightened and bolts, but it is not yet gored.

The other large plate, handled with a ferocious technique in which the etching needle dances and careens over the surface with the greatest freedom and even abandon, uses the bull ring as a setting for unleashed violence. Here the bull is impaled upon a picador's lance and the horse starts in fear of the maddened bull. Between these two animals is the greatly distorted figure of the partly dressed woman. In this print she is in a languid twisted swoon, oblivious to the frenzy and violence literally supporting her. She is a kind of dream of indolent sensuality, buoyed up by the highest passion and most intense feeling, but yet apart from them. At the left, there is another personage costumed for the ring, skipping and dancing in a posture of alarm and excitement. Tiers of spectators are roughly indicated in their arcaded seats or behind the barricade and at the extreme upper right a classical head of a woman, filleted with flowers, gazes over all with a sad and enigmatic expression. She is the muse or genius, an emblem of sentient vitality, who Picasso chooses to preside at his elemental dramas. She passively observes, taking no part in the action, and the suggestion of regret in her expression seems to indicate that the most horrific present and incidental reality barely disturbs the surface of a timeless absorption in higher verities.

Despite the enormous outpouring of energy involved in preparation for the execution of *Guernica* in the early summer of 1937, several important prints were executed in that year and in 1938. The large and spectacular *Combat* drypoint of 1937, the artist's only specific treatment of armed violence during the wars beginning to engulf Europe, is surpassed only by the great *Weeping Woman* of the same year, the graphic counterpart to the famous painting in the Penrose Collection.

In 1938 Picasso turns again to aquatint (used together with etching as did Goya) to produce the incomparable *Woman with a Tambourine*. This huge plate shows the nude female musician in a frenzy of music and dance. Her figure moves and sways in vigorous and propulsive rhythms.

The Second World War of course necessitated a reduction of artistic activity for Picasso, though he nevertheless managed to keep his production at a surprisingly large volume. The delightful plates of the Buffon *Histoire Naturelle* series, one of the last projects intended to be carried out with Vollard, are the single greatest printmaking accomplishment of Picasso in the years 1939-1945. These elegant and amusing plates, executed during a single month in 1942, show nothing of the conflict raging over the world, and the love of nature and animals expressed in them, through a fresh and ingenious use of aquatint and drypoint, seem to have been for Picasso an escape from the frightful realities of wartime existence.

Not long after the conclusion of the war Picasso turns again to printmaking on a large scale, both in terms of the volume of his production and the impressive size of the works. Utilizing the expert facilities of Mourlot Frères he took up lithography with a startling enthusiasm that would appear to have been building up during the war. While Picasso had made lithographs earlier, the medium of lithography was not one that he often turned to for major statements. In all he had produced but twenty-eight lithographs before 1945. In the five years from 1945 through 1950, however, the artist produced nearly two hundred lithographs, many of which exist in numerous states, each so elaborately worked that they must be counted as separate and distinct artistic endeavors. The ten states of the *Head of a Young Woman* of 1945 and the eighteen states of the *Two Female Nudes* executed in 1945-1946 indicate the degree of absorption in lithography which Picasso permitted himself in addition to very prolific production in painting, drawing, and sculpture. To date, Picasso has produced nearly five hundred lithographs, utilizing practically all imaginable potentialities of the meduim. He has drawn directly on the stone or zinc with brush, pencil and crayon and used transfer drawings. The images have been refined with scraping, acid work and redrawing. Large and complex prints in as many as six or eight colors have demonstrated complete mastery of the difficult problems of design and registry within monumental compositions such as the great *Figure in a Striped Blouse* of 1952. The image conceived as relieved in white against the rich ground of the superb inks Picasso employs resulted in such masterpieces as the famous *Dove* of 1950, and the extraordinary series of ten variations on a *David and Bathsheba* by Cranach the Elder. The flexibility characteristic of lithography seems to appeal greatly to Picasso, who has exploited it for the greatest variety of undertakings, from sober conceptions which compete with his paintings in gravity and impact to informal productions of charming spontaneity for posters, whimsies, and all manner of *pièces d'occasion*.

Despite the volume of his lithographic production, Picasso has not neglected other print media, and since the war has had conspicuous success with the sugar-ground aquatint and related techniques, which have permitted him to paint the image directly on the plate with all the flickering brio of his magnificent late brush drawings. The groups of *Corrida* subjects, and the large and ambitious plates of the artist with models and motley visitors in the studio are the best known of these. Successive bitings, roulette work, and other virtuoso methods enliven these frequently large plates through the entire range of subjects the artist has been moved to approach.

Still more recently, the artist has turned to yet another medium as the outlet for his phenomenal creative energies, the linoleum cut. This simple technique, familiar to nearly everyone from art and craft classes in elementary school or camp, Picasso has transformed into a medium of the greatest sophistication and complexity by daring innovations and surpassing skill. The most brilliant of these linoleum cuts use many colors, enlarging the normal range of expression of the medium considerably, and they do so without submitting to the necessity of a separate block for each color. Picasso managed to do this by the exceptional notion of devising a kind of "stopping out," wherein the block, with some preliminary cutting and inking in the usual fashion, has paper templates laid over portions of it before printing. The resulting impression will have corresponding white areas which have been achieved without cutting into those portions of the block, as would ordinarily be required. These uncut portions may then later be cut and inked in different colors and the block printed again on the same impression, usually once for each color (depending on the composition), until the desired result has been achieved. Besides the gains in the flexibility and expressiveness of the technique, there is a great saving in time and labor, and the always vexing problems of registry are considerably simplified. Several compositions involving a still life seen under an electric lamp, and the *Bust of a Girl Inspired by Cranach* exemplify this late flowering of Picasso's printmaking abilities at its very greatest.

Midway in his eighth decade, Picasso continues to produce prints of exceptional quality. The verve and intensity of this continuing creativity has come to have something of the miraculous about it, mysterious in its sources and awesome in its fullness. Perhaps it is most accurate to consider this phenomenom and its meaning as one and the same, and as far beyond the relevance of analysis as a force of nature. DENNIS ADRIAN

95

108   The Frugal Repast, 1904. The Alfred Stieglitz Collection

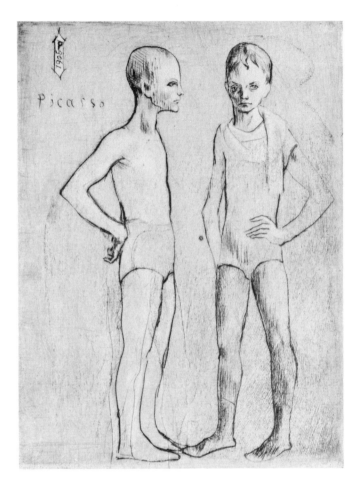

109   *Two Saltimbanques, 1905.*
The Albert Roullier Memorial Collection

114   *Bust of a Young Woman, 1906.*
Gift of The Print and Drawing Club

97

115　*Still Life with Bottle (Vie Marc), 1912. The John H. Wrenn Memorial Collection*

120   *The Artist Before his Painting, 1927.*
       Print and Drawing Purchase Fund

133   *Sculptor and Model by a Window, 1933.*
       Lent by Mr. and Mrs. Everett Kovler

125 *Satyr and Sleeping Woman, 1933. Lent by Dr. Eugene A. Solow*

138   *Dying Minotaur, 1933. Print and Drawing Purchase Fund*   128   *The Embrace, 1933. Anonymous Gift*

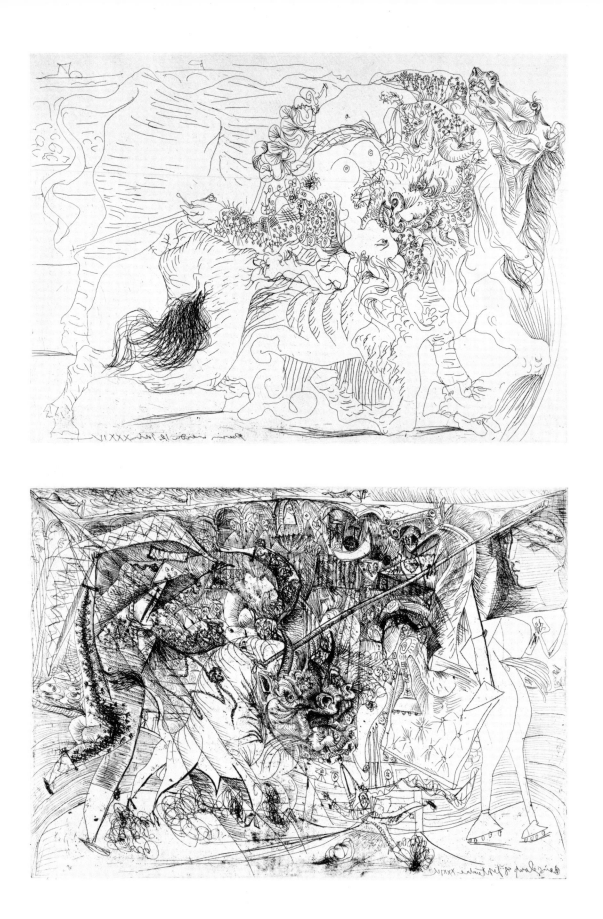

140 *Left above, Tauromachia, 1934. Bequest of Curt Valentin*
141 *Left below, Tauromachia, 1934. Bequest of Curt Valentin*
142 *Above, Minotauromachia, 1935. Gift of Mrs. P. Donnelley*

143   *Blind Minotaur Led through the Night, ca. 1935. Lent by Dr. Eugene A. Solow*

144 *Boy Watching a Sleeping Woman*
     by Candlelight, ca. 1935.
     Lent by Mr. and Mrs. Everett Kovler

145 *Four Children Looking at a Monster,*
     ca. 1938. Gift of
     Mr. and Mrs. Samuel E. Johnson

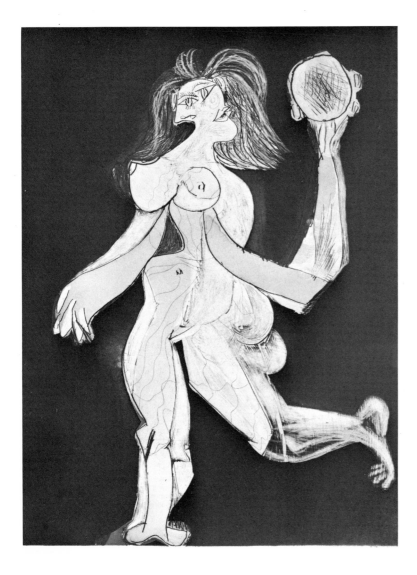

149   *The Tambourine Player, 1938. Print and Drawing Purchase Fund*

152   *Ostrich, 1942. Print and Drawing Purchase*

161   *Femme assisse et dormeuse, 1947. Gift of The Print and Drawing Club*

162   *David and Bathsheba (after Cranach), 1948. Lent by Mr. and Mrs. Morton G. Neumann*

165 *The Dove, 1949.*
    Gift of The Print and Drawing Club

169 *Young Girl Inspired by Cranach, 1949.*
    Gift of Mr. and Mrs. Joseph R. Shapiro

170   *Figure in a Striped Blouse, 1949.*
        Gift of Mr. and Mrs. Morton G. Neumann

174   *Woman at a Window, 1952.*
        Lent by Mr. and Mrs. Morton G. Neumann

181   Jacqueline, 1958. Gift of Mr. and Mrs. Leigh B. Block

Catalogue of the Exhibition

Paintings

Measurements for paintings are given in both inches and centimeters, and for drawings and prints in millimeters. Height precedes width. References cited most frequently are abbreviated as follows:

B.=Bolliger, Hans. *Picasso for Vollard*, New York, 1956 (?)
G.=Geiser, Bernhard. *Picasso, Peintre-Graveur*, Berne, 1933
M.=Mourlot, Fernand. *Picasso Lithographe*, Monte Carlo, 1949
Zervos=Zervos, Christian. *Pablo Picasso*, Paris, 1932-

1   Young Woman
Paris, 1900. Pastel on board. Size: 14⅛ x 10¼ in. (36 x 26 cm.) (sight). *Bibl.*: P. Daix and G. Boudaille, *Picasso, The Blue and Rose Periods, A Catalogue Raisonné 1900-1906*, transl. by Phoebe Pool, Greenwich, Conn., 1966, Cat. No. II.22, repr. p. 125. *Ex coll.*: Joseph Winterbotham, Chicago
Owned by The Art Institute of Chicago, Gift of Joseph Winterbotham, 1954.319

2   Nude with Cats
Paris, 1901. Oil on cardboard. Size: 17½ x 16 in. (44.5 x 40.8 cm.). Signed lower right: Picasso. *Bibl.*: C. Zervos, *Pablo Picasso*, I, Paris, 1932, No. 93, repr. pl. 46; P. Daix and G. Boudaille, *Picasso, The Blue and Rose Periods, A Catalogue Raisonné 1900-1906*, transl. by Phoebe Pool, Greenwich, Conn., 1966, Cat. No. V.16, repr. p. 166. *Ex coll.*: Paul Guillaume, Paris; Reinhardt Galleries, New York
Owned by The Art Institute of Chicago, The Amy McCormick Memorial Collection, 1942.464

3   Peonies
Paris, 1901. Oil on canvas. Size: 23 x 15½ in. (57 x 38 cm.). Signed lower right: Picasso. *Bibl.*: C. Zervos, *Pablo Picasso*, I, Paris, 1932, No. 60, repr. pl. 28; P. Daix and G. Boudaille, *Picasso, The Blue and Rose Periods, A Catalogue Raisonné 1900-1906*, transl. by Phoebe Pool, Greenwich, Conn., 1966, Cat. No. V.23, repr. p. 168. *Ex coll.*: Le marquis de Biron; Chester H. Johnson, Chicago; Mrs. Charles B. Goodspeed, Chicago (presently Mrs. Gilbert W. Chapman, New York)
Lent by Mrs. Gilbert W. Chapman, New York

4   On the Upper Deck (The Omnibus)
Paris, 1901. Oil on cardboard mounted on cradled wool panel. Size: 19⅜ x 25¼ in. (49.2 x 64.2 cm.). Signed lower right: Picasso. *Bibl.*: P. Daix and G. Boudaille, *Picasso, The Blue and Rose Periods, A Catalogue Raisonné 1900-1906*, transl, by Phoebe Pool, Greenwich, Conn., 1966, Cat. No. V.61, repr. p. 182. *Ex coll.*: Howard Young, New York; Mrs. A. S. Coburn, Chicago
Owned by The Art Institute of Chicago, Mr. and Mrs. Lewis L. Coburn Memorial Collection, 1933.448

5   Women and Child at the Fountain
Paris, 1901. Oil on canvas. Size: 36½ x 28¼ in. (81 x 65 cm.). Signed upper right: Picasso. *Bibl.*: C. Zervos, *Pablo Picasso*, I, Paris, 1932, No. 80, repr. pl. 40; P. Daix and G. Boudaille, *Picasso, The Blue and Rose Periods, A Catalogue Raisonné 1900-1906*, transl. by Phoebe Pool, Greenwich, Conn., 1966, Cat. No. VI.10, repr. p. 196. *Ex coll.*: Potter Palmer, Chicago
Lent Anonymously

6   Woman with Folded Arms
Barcelona, 1902. Oil on fabric. Size: 31⅞ x 23 in. (81 x 58.5 cm.). Signed upper left: Picasso. *Bibl.*: C. Zervos, *Pablo Picasso*, I, Paris, 1932, No. 105, repr. pl. 52, (dated 1901); *Picasso "Blue" and "Rose" Periods, 1901-1906*, Jacques Seligmann & Co., Inc., New York, November 2-November 26, 1936, Cat. No. 9, repr. frontispiece; C. Zervos, *Pablo Picasso*, VI (supplement to I-V), Paris, 1954, No. 543, repr. pl. 67, (dated 1903); P. Daix and G. Boudaille, *Picasso, The Blue and Rose Periods, A Catalogue Raisonné 1900-1906*, transl. by Phoebe Pool, Greenwich, Conn., 1966, Cat. No. VII.7, repr. p. 208, (dated Barcelona, 1902). *Ex coll.*: Stein, Paris; Moser; Baron G., Berlin; Mr. and Mrs. Chauncey McCormick, Chicago
Lent by Roger McCormick

7   The Old Guitarist
Barcelona, 1903. Oil on panel (wood mounted on masonite). Size: 48⅛ x 32⁷⁄₁₆ in. (122.3 x 82.5 cm.). Signed lower right: Picasso. *Bibl.*: C. Zervos, *Pablo Picasso*, I, Paris, 1932, No. 202, repr. pl. 90; P. Daix and G. Boudaille, *Picasso, The Blue and Rose Periods, A Catalogue Raisonné 1900-1906*, transl. by Phoebe Pool, Greenwich, Conn., 1966, Cat. No. IX.34, repr. p. 229. *Ex coll.*: Ambroise Vollard, Paris; John Quinn, New York; Frederick C. Bartlett, Chicago
Owned by The Art Institute of Chicago, Helen Birch Bartlett Memorial Collection, 1926.253

8   Woman with a Helmet of Hair
Paris, 1904. Gouache on paperboard. Size: 16⅞ x 12¼ in. (42.9 x 31.2 cm.). Signed and dated, upper left: Picasso/1904. *Bibl.*: C. Zervos, *Pablo Picasso*, I, Paris, 1932, No. 233, repr. pl. 103; P. Daix and G. Boudaille, *Picasso, The Blue and Rose Periods, A Catalogue Raisonné 1900-1906*, transl. by Phoebe Pool, Greenwich, Conn., 1966, Cat. No. XI.7, repr. p. 240, p. 237 (color). *Ex coll.*: Alfred Gold, Berlin; Chester H. Johnson, Chicago; Mr. and Mrs. Walter S. Brewster, Chicago
Owned by The Art Institute of Chicago, Gift of Kate L. Brewster, 1950.128

9   Nude with Pitcher
Summer, 1906. Oil on canvas. Size: 39⅜ x 32 in. (100 x 81 cm.). Signed lower right: Picasso. *Bibl.*: C. Zervos, *Pablo Picasso*, I, Paris, 1932, No. 330, repr. pl. 154, (dated 1905); P. Daix and G. Boudaille, *Picasso, The Blue and Rose Periods, A Catalogue Raisonné 1900-1906*, transl. by Phoebe Pool, Greenwich, Conn., 1966, Cat. No. XV.23, repr. p. 298, (dated summer, 1906); J. Rewald, *100 European Paintings & Drawings from the Collection of Mr. and Mrs. Leigh B. Block* [exhibition catalogue], National Gallery of Art and Los Angeles County Museum of Art, 1967, Cat. No. 36, repr., (dated 1906). *Ex coll.*: Dr. G. F. Reber, Lausanne; Alfred Richet, Paris; Edward James, London
Lent by Mr. and Mrs. Leigh B. Block

10   Bust of Woman
Paris, autumn 1906. Oil on canvas board. Size: 31½ x 25¼ in. (80.2 x 64.2 cm.). Signed upper right (considerably later): Picasso. *Bibl.*: C. Zervos, *Pablo Picasso*, I, Paris, 1932, No. 374, repr. pl. 179; *Picasso, Peintures 1900-1955*, Musée des Arts Décoratifs, Paris, June-October 1955, Cat. No. 13, repr.; P. Daix and G. Boudaille, *Picasso, The Blue and Rose Periods, A Catalogue Raisonné 1900-1906*, transl. by Phoebe Pool, Greenwich, Conn., 1966, Cat. No. XVI.24. repr. p. 326. *Ex coll.*: Paul Guillaume, Paris; Valentine Gallery, New York; Walter P. Chrysler, Jr., New York; Mr. and Mrs. Samuel A. Marx, Chicago

Owned by The Art Institute of Chicago, Gift of Florene May Schoenborn and Samuel A. Marx, 1959.619

11 Seated Nude
Paris, summer 1909. Gouache on illustration board. Size: 24¾ x 19 in. (68 x 48.3 cm.). Signed lower right in pencil and lower left in ink: Picasso. *Bibl.:* C. Zervos, *Pablo Picasso,* II Part 1, Paris, 1942, No. 154, repr. pl. 76. *Ex coll.:* Galerie Pierre, Paris; Mr. and Mrs. Samuel A. Marx, Chicago
Owned by The Art Institute of Chicago, Gift of Florene May Schoenborn and Samuel A. Marx, 1953.192

12 Head of a Woman
Horta de San Juan (also called Horta de Ebro), summer 1909. Oil on canvas. Size: 23⅞ x $20\frac{3}{16}$ in. (60.8 x 51.3 cm.). *Bibl.:* C. Zervos, *Pablo Picasso,* II part 1, Paris, 1942, No. 167, repr. pl. 83. *Ex coll.:* Dr. G. F. Reber, Lausanne; Valentine Gallery, New York; Joseph Winterbotham, Chicago
Owned by The Art Institute of Chicago, The Joseph Winterbotham Collection, 1940.5

13 Woman Sewing
Paris, spring 1910. Oil on canvas. Size: 31½ x 24½ in. (80 x 62.2 cm.). Signed upper left: Picasso. *Bibl.:* C. Zervos, *Pablo Picasso,* II part 1, Paris, 1942, No. 199, repr. pl. 99. *Ex coll.:* Walter P. Chrysler, Jr., New York
Lent by Mrs. Ernest Zeisler

14 Girl with Raised Left Arm
Paris, spring 1910. Oil on canvas. Size: 21⅝ x 18⅛ in. (55 x 46 cm.). *Bibl.:* C. Zervos, *Pablo Picasso,* II part 1, Paris, 1942, No. 216, repr. pl. 106. *Ex coll.:* Wilhelm Uhde, Paris
Lent by Mr. and Mrs. Morton G. Neumann

15 Woman with Mandolin
Cadaquès, summer 1910. Oil on canvas. Size: 36 x 24¼ in. (91.5 x 61.5 cm.). Signed and dated, on back of canvas. *Bibl.:* C. Zervos, *Pablo Picasso,* II part 1, Paris, 1942, No. 222, repr. pl. 110. *Ex coll.:* Ambroise Vollard, Paris
Lent by Mr. and Mrs. Roy Friedman

16 Daniel-Henry Kahnweiler
Paris, autumn 1910. Oil on canvas. Size: 39⅝ x 28⅝ in. (100.6 x 72.8 cm.). *Bibl.:* C. Zervos, *Pablo Picasso,* II part 1, Paris, 1942, No. 227, repr. pl. 113. *Ex coll.:* Galerie Simon, Paris (?); Mrs. Charles B. Goodspeed, Chicago (presently Mrs. Gilbert W. Chapman, New York)
Owned by The Art Institute of Chicago, Gift of Mrs. Gilbert W. Chapman in memory of Charles B. Goodspeed, 1948.561

17 Woman
Paris, autumn 1910. Oil on canvas. Size: 39⅜ x 31⅞ in. (100 x 81 cm.). *Bibl.:* C. Zervos, *Pablo Picasso,* II part 1, Paris, 1942, No. 234, repr. pl. 116, *Ex coll.:* Earl Horter Collection; Mrs. Charles B. Goodspeed, Chicago (presently Mrs. Gilbert W. Chapman, New York)
Lent by Mrs. Gilbert W. Chapman, New York

18 Still Life with Matches, Pipe, and Glass
Paris, autumn 1911. Oil on canvas. Size: 8¾ x 4¾ in. (22 x 12 cm.). *Bibl.:* C. Zervos, *Pablo Picasso,* II part 1, Paris, 1942, No. 284, repr. pl. 138. *Ex coll.:* Jean Coutrot, Paris
Collection of Mr. and Mrs. James W. Alsdorf

19 Glass
Paris, spring 1912. Oil on canvas. Size: 12⅝ x $6\frac{11}{16}$ in. (32 x 17 cm.). *Bibl.:* C. Zervos, *Pablo Picasso,* II part 2, Paris, 1942, No. 731, repr. pl. 320
Lent by Mrs. Ernest Zeisler

20 "Au Bon Marché"
Paris, winter 1912-1913. Collage and oil on cardboard. Size: $12\frac{3}{16}$ x 9¼ in. (31 x 23.5 cm.). Signed on back. *Bibl.:* J. Cassou, *Picasso,* transl. by Mary Chamot, London, New York, Paris, 1940, p. 88, repr.; C. Zervos, *Pablo Picasso,* II part 2, Paris, 1942, No. 378, repr. pl. 183; *Picasso,* Musée de Lyon, 1953, Cat. No. 28, repr. fig. 9. *Ex coll.:* D. H. Kahnweiler, Paris; Mr. M. G. Bollag, Zurich
Lent by Mr. and Mrs. Michael Newbury

21 Bottle of "Marc de Bourgogne," Glass, Newspaper
Paris, spring 1913. Oil and collage on canvas. Size: 18⅛ x 15 in. (46 x 38 cm.). Inscribed on back of canvas: Sur une table ronde/ une bouteille de marc de Bourgogne/un verre et un journal au fond/une glace/1913/ Picasso. *Bibl.:* C. Zervos, *Pablo Picasso,* II part 2, Paris, 1942, No. 432, repr. pl. 202. *Ex coll.:* D.-H. Kahnweiler, Paris; Sara Lewis
Lent by Mr. and Mrs. B. E. Bensinger

22 Glass
Avignon, summer 1914. Collage, oil and gouache on paper. Size: 10¾ x 9⅝ in. (27.3 x 24.4 cm.). Signed lower left: Picasso. *Bibl.:* C. Zervos, *Pablo Picasso,* II part 2, Paris, 1942, No. 462, repr. pl. 215. *Ex coll.:* Roland Penrose, London
Collection of Mr. and Mrs. James W. Alsdorf

23 Man with a Pipe
Paris, 1915. Oil on canvas. Size: 51¼ x 35¼ in. (130.3 x 89.5 cm.). Signed lower right: Picasso 15. *Bibl.: Pablo Picasso,* Wadsworth Atheneum, Hartford, Conn., February 6-March 1, 1934, Cat. No. 30; C. Zervos, *Pablo Picasso,* II part 2, Paris, 1942, No. 654, repr. pl. 261, (dated Paris, 1916). *Ex coll.:* Errazuriz, Paris; Rolf de Maré, Paris
Owned by The Art Institute of Chicago, Gift of Mrs. Leigh B. Block in memory of Albert D. Lasker, 1952.1116

24 Still Life
1918. Oil on panel. Size: 7¼ x 9½ in. (18.4 x 24.1 cm.). Signed upper left: Picasso. *Ex coll.:* Galerie Etienne Bignou, Paris
Lent by Mr. and Mrs. Roy Friedman

25 Mother and Child
1921. Oil on canvas. Size: 56½ x 64 in. (143.5 x 162.6 cm.). Signed lower right: Picasso/21. *Bibl.:* C. Zervos, *Pablo Picasso,* IV, Paris, 1951, No. 311, repr. pl. 115. *Ex coll.:* Dr. G. F. Reber, Lausanne; Paul Rosenberg, New York
Owned by The Art Institute of Chicago, Gift of Mary and Leigh Block Charitable Fund, Inc., Mr. and Mrs. Edwin E. Hokin, Maymar Corporation, Mr. and Mrs. Chauncey McCormick, Mrs. Maurice L. Rothschild, and the Ada Turnbull Hertle Fund, 1954.270

26 Still Life
February 4, 1922. Oil on canvas. Size: 32¼ x 39½ in. (81.6 x 100.3 cm.). Dated upper left: 4-2-22-. *Ex coll.:* Gertrude Stein; M. Knoedler & Company, New York; Culberg, Chicago
Owned by The Art Institute of Chicago, Ada Turnbull Hertle Fund, 1953.28

27 Still Life with Bread, Glass, Camembert, Knife
Dinard, 1922. Oil on canvas. Size: 8¾ x 10¾ in. (22.2 x 27.3 cm.). Signed upper left: Picasso. *Bibl.:* C. Zervos, *Pablo Picasso,* IV, Paris, 1951, No. 399, repr. pl. 167
Lent by Mr. and Mrs. Leigh B. Block

28 Harlequin
1923. Oil on canvas. Size: 18⅛ x $14\frac{15}{16}$ in. (46 x 38 cm.). Signed upper left: Picasso/23. *Bibl.:* M. Dale, *Picasso,* New York, 1930, No. 30, repr.; C. Zervos, *Pablo Picasso,* V, Paris, 1952, No. 62, repr. pl. 35. *Ex coll.:* Samuel Courtauld, London
Lent by Mrs. Ernest Zeisler

29 Bust of a Woman
1923. Oil on canvas. Size: 25¾ x 21¼ in. (65 x 34 cm.). Signed lower left: Picasso. *Bibl.: Picasso,* Statements by Pablo Picasso, Preface by Alfred H. Barr, Jr., Commentaries by Roland Penrose, Editions Beyeler, Basle, 1967-1968, No. 34, repr. p. 59
Lent by Mr. and Mrs. B. E. Bensinger

30 Seated Woman
1924. Oil on canvas. Size: 13 x $9\frac{7}{16}$ in. (33 x 24 cm.). Signed and dated, bottom right: 24/Picasso. Dated on the stretcher: 1924. *Bibl.:* C. Zervos, *Pablo Picasso,* V. Paris, 1952, No. 272, repr. pl. 128
Lent Anonymously

31 Head
Cannes, 1927. Oil and plaster on canvas. Size: $39\frac{3}{16}$ x 31¾ in. (99.4 x 80.8 cm.). *Bibl.:* C. Zervos, *Pablo Picasso,* VII, Paris, 1955, No. 118, repr. pl. 51. *Ex coll.:* The artist; André Breton; Gordon Onslow-Ford; Mr. and Mrs. Samuel A. Marx, Chicago
Owned by The Art Institute of Chicago, Gift of Florene May Schoenborn and Samuel A. Marx, 1951.185

32 Head
1928. Oil on canvas and sand. Size: 21⅝ x 13 in. (55 x 33 cm.). Signed upper left: Picasso. *Bibl.:* C. Zervos, *Pablo Picasso,* VII, Paris, 1955, No. 121, repr. pl. 52
Lent by Mrs. Ernest Zeisler

33 Woman, Sculpture and Vase of Flowers
Paris, April 24, 1929. Oil on canvas. Size: 76¾ x $51\frac{3}{16}$ in. (195 x 130 cm.). Signed lower left: Picasso/29. *Bibl.:* C. Zervos, *Pablo Picasso,* VII, Paris, 1955, No. 259, repr. pl. 105. *Ex coll.:* The artist; Galerie Pierre Loeb, Paris
Lent by Mr. and Mrs. Nathan Cummings

34 Abstraction: Background with Blue Cloudy Sky
January 4, 1930. Oil on cradled wood panel. Size: 26 x 19⅜ in. (66.1 x 49.4 cm.). Signed and dated, lower right: Picasso/4-I-xxx. *Bibl.:* C. Zervos, *Pablo Picasso,* VII, Paris, 1955, No. 304, repr. pl. 124. *Ex coll.:* W. Rees Jeffreys, Wivelsfield Green, Sussex; A. Zwemmer, Ltd., London
Owned by The Art Institute of Chicago, Gift of Florene May Schoenborn and Samuel A. Marx and the Wilson L. Mead Fund, 1955.748

35 The Red Armchair
December 16, 1931. Oil and ripolin (enamel) on plywood. 51½ x 39 in. (130.9 x 99.2 cm.). Signed upper right (since 1955): Picasso. Dated on back. *Bibl.:* C. Zervos, *Pablo Picasso,* VII, Paris, 1955, No. 334, repr. pl. 139; *Picasso, Peintures 1900-1955,* Musée des Arts Décoratifs, Paris, June-October 1955, Cat. No. 76, repr. *Ex coll.:* The artist; Mr. and Mrs. Daniel Saidenberg, New York
Owned by The Art Institute of Chicago, Gift of Mr. and Mrs. Daniel Saidenberg, 1957.72

36 Woman with a Flower
April 10, 1932. Oil on canvas. Size: 63¾ x 51¼ in. (161.9 x 130.2 cm.). Signed lower right: Picasso. *Bibl.:* C. Zervos, *Pablo Picasso,* VII, Paris, 1955, No. 381, repr. pl. 169. *Ex coll.:* Walter P. Chrysler, Jr., New York; M. Knoedler & Company, New York; G. David Thompson, Pittsburgh
Lent by Mr. and Mrs. Nathan Cummings

37 Girl Writing
1934. Oil on canvas, Size: 63⅞ x 51⅜ in. (162.5 x 130.5 cm.). Signed and dated, upper right: Picasso/XXXIV. *Bibl.:* C. Zervos, *Pablo Picasso,* VIII, Paris, 1957, No. 246, repr. pl. 114. *Ex coll.:* Peter Watson; Mr. and Mrs. Samuel A. Marx, Chicago
Lent by Florene M. Schoenborn

38 Portrait of Dora Maar
Paris, April 1, 1939. Oil on canvas. 36½ x 29 in. (92.7 x 73.7). Dated on back. *Bibl.:* C. Zervos, *Pablo Picasso,* IX, Paris, 1958, No. 282, repr. pl. 131. *Ex coll.:* Mlle Dora Maar, Paris
Lent by Mr. and Mrs. Edwin A. Bergman

39 Head of a Woman
April 11, 1940. Oil on canvas. Size: 28¾ x 21⅜ in. (73 x 54.3 cm.) (trimmed). Signed lower left: Picasso/11.4.40. *Bibl.:* C. Zervos, *Pablo Picasso,* X, Paris, 1959, No. 384, repr. pl. 127
Lent by the Alsdorf Foundation

40 Seated Woman
October 9, 1941. Oil on canvas. Size: $45\frac{11}{16}$ x $35\frac{1}{16}$ in. (116 x 89 cm.). Signed lower right (since 1960): Picasso. *Bibl.:* C. Zervos, *Pablo Picasso,* XI, Paris, 1960, No. 333, repr. pl. 129
Lent by Mr. and Mrs. Morton G. Neumann

41 Still Life with Basket of Cherries
June 16, 1943. Oil on canvas. Size: 24 x 18⅛ in. (61 x 46 cm.). Signed lower right: Picasso. *Bibl.:* C. Zervos, *Pablo Picasso,* XIII, Paris, 1962, No. 54, repr. pl. 27
Lent by Mr. and Mrs. Michael Newbury

42 Chair with Gladiolas
Paris, September 17, 1943. Oil on canvas. Size: 56¾ x 44½ in. (146 x 114 cm.). Signed upper right (since 1946): Picasso. Dated on back. *Bibl.:* A. H. Barr, Jr., Picasso: *Fifty Years of his Art,* The Museum of Modern Art, New York, 1946, p. 236, repr.; C. Zervos, *Pablo Picasso,* XIII, Paris, 1962, No. 123, repr. pl. 67. *Ex coll.:* The artist
Lent by Mr. and Mrs. Leigh B. Block

43 Woman with Cat
1944. Oil on canvas. Size: 50½ x 37½ in. (128.3 x 94.6 cm.). Signed lower left: Picasso. *Bibl.: Picasso, His Later Works, 1938-1961,* Worcester Art Museum, January 25-February 25, 1962, Cat. No. 9, repr. p. 15. *Ex coll.:* Mr. and Mrs. Leigh B. Block, Chicago
Lent by Mr. and Mrs. Willard Gidwitz

44 The Vase of Flowers
May 26, 1947 and July 11, 1948. Oil on canvas. Size: 15 x 12 in. (38.1 x 30.5 cm.). Signed lower left: Picasso. *Bibl.:* C. Zervos, *Pablo Picasso,* XV, Paris, 1965, No. 98, repr. pl. 55
Lent Anonymously

45 Still Life with Pitcher and Candlestick
January 29, 1945 and December 22, 1946. Oil on canvas. Size: 18 x 21½ in. (45.7 x 54.6 cm.). Signed upper right (since 1963): Picasso, and dated lower left (since 1963): 29.1.45. Dated on back of canvas: 29—1. 45./(II)/22. D. 46. *Bibl.:* C. Zervos, *Pablo Picasso,* XIV, Paris, 1963, No. 67, repr. pl. 32, (first version), and No. 131, repr. pl. 61, (final version). *Ex coll.:* Perls Galleries, New York
Lent by the Alsdorf Foundation

46 Seated Woman
February 20, 1949. Oil on canvas. Size: 45½ x 35 in. (115.6 x 88.9 cm.). Dated upper left: 20.2.49, and signed upper left (since 1965): Picasso. *Bibl.:* C. Zervos, *Pablo Picasso,* XV, Paris, 1965, No. 123, repr. pl. 71
Lent by Mr. and Mrs. Albert Newman

47 Head of a Woman
1949. Oil on canvas. Size: 9 x 6 in. (22.8 x 15.2 cm.). Signed bottom right: Picasso. *Bibl.:* C. Zervos, *Pablo Picasso,* XV, Paris, 1965, No. 148, repr. pl. 90
Lent Anonymously

48 Villa and Palm Tree
1951. Oil on canvas. Size: 15 x 18⅛ in. (38 x 46 cm.). Signed lower left: Picasso. *Bibl.:* C. Zervos, *Pablo Picasso,* XV, Paris, 1965, No. 188, repr. pl. 111
Collection of Mr. and Mrs. James W. Alsdorf

49 The Reader
Vallauris, January 29, 1953. Oil on canvas mounted on plywood panel. Size: 36¼ x 28⅝ in. (92.1 x 72.8 cm.). Signed upper right: Picasso. *Bibl.:* C. Zervos, *Pablo Picasso,* XV, Paris, 1965, No. 234, repr. pl. 134. *Ex coll.:* Mrs. Margit Chanin, New York
Owned by The Art Institute of Chicago, Gift of Mr. and Mrs. Arnold H. Maremont through the Kate Maremont Foundation, 1956.336

50 Woman with Scarf
March 6, 1953. Oil on canvas. Size: 36¼ x 28¾ in. (92 x 73 cm.). Signed lower right: Picasso. *Bibl.:* C. Zervos, *Pablo Picasso,* XV, Paris, 1965, No. 240, repr. pl. 136, (described as oil on plywood)
Lent by Mr. and Mrs. Louis N. Cohen

51 Sylvette
Vallauris, April 19, May 22, and October 4, 1954. Oil on canvas. Size: 51½ x 38¼ in. (130.9 x 97.2 cm.). Signed upper left: Picasso. Dated on back. *Bibl.:* C. Zervos, *Pablo Picasso,* XVI, Paris, 1965, No. 315, repr. pl. 105, (described as oil on wood panel)
Owned by The Art Institute of Chicago, Gift of Mr. and Mrs. Leigh B. Block, 1955.821

52 Bust of a Woman in Colors
March 27, 1956 (II). Oil on canvas. Size: 28¾ x 23⅝ in. (73 x 60 cm.). Signed upper left: Picasso. *Bibl.:* C. Zervos, *Pablo Picasso,* XVII, Paris, 1966, No. 51, repr. pl. 20
Lent Anonymously

53 Bullfight
Cannes, April 27, 1956 (I). Oil on canvas. Size: 18⅛ x 21⅝ in. (46 x 55 cm.). Signed bottom right: Picasso, and dated upper right: 27.4.56. Dated on back of canvas: 27.4.56./I. *Bibl.:* C. Zervos, *Pablo Picasso,* XVII, Paris, 1966, No. 93, repr. pl. 41
Lent Anonymously

54 Nude Under a Pine Tree
Vauvenargues, January 20, 1959. Oil on canvas. Size: 76½ x 110 in. (195 x 280 cm.). Signed lower right: Picasso. *Bibl.:* C. Zervos, *Pablo Picasso,* XVIII, Paris, 1967, No. 323, repr. pl. 93
Ex coll.: Galerie Louise Leiris, Paris
Owned by The Art Institute of Chicago, Grant J. Pick Collection, 1965.687

55 Woman by the Side of a Stream
1960. Oil on canvas. Size: 19⅝ x 24 in. (49.9 x 61 cm.). Signed upper right: Picasso. *Bibl.: Pablo Picasso Exhibition—Japan 1964,* Tokyo National Museum of Modern Art, Kyoto National Museum of Modern Art, Nagoya Prefectural Museum, 1964, Cat. No. 139, repr.
Lent by Mr. and Mrs. Henry Markus

56 Bust of Woman with Hat
January 4 and April 12, 1962. Oil on canvas. Size: 57½ x 44⅞ in. (146 x 114 cm.). Signed lower left: Picasso. *Bibl.: Picasso, Peintures 1962-1963,* Galerie Louise Leiris, Paris, January 15-February 15, 1964, Cat. No. 2, repr. p. 10. *Ex coll.:* Galerie Louise Leiris, Paris
Lent by Mr. and Mrs. Edwin E. Hokin

57 Woman with Dog
November 21, 1962 (II). Oil on canvas. Size: 63¾ x 51⅜ in. (162 x 130 cm.). Signed upper right: Picasso, and dated upper left: 21.11.62. *Bibl.: Picasso, Peintures 1962-1963,* Galerie Louise Leiris, Paris, January 15-February 15, 1964, Cat. No. 13, repr. p. 18. *Ex coll.:* Galerie Louise Leiris, Paris
Lent by Mr. and Mrs. Nathan Cummings

58 Woman with Mirror
January 8, 1963. Oil on canvas. Size: $45\frac{11}{16}$ x $35\frac{1}{16}$ in. (116 x 89 cm.). Signed upper right: Picasso. *Bibl.: Picasso, Peintures 1962-1963,* Galerie Louise Leiris, Paris, January 15-February 15, 1964, Cat. No. 16, repr. p. 20. *Ex coll.:* Galerie Louise Leiris, Paris
Lent by Mr. and Mrs. Henry Markus

Drawings

59   At the Cabaret, ca. 1898-1900
Colored crayons, 125 x 214 mm
The Lewis L. Coburn Memorial Collection. 33.527

60   Two Figure Studies, 1904
Pen and black ink, 252 x 333 mm. Zervos VI, no. 628
Gift of Robert Allerton. 23.1058

61   Study of a Seated Man, ca. 1905
Pencil, 329 x 215 mm
Gift of Robert Allerton. 24.803

62   Female Nude seen from the Back, ca. 1906
Black chalk, 316 x 249 mm
Gift of Walter S. Brewster. 54.1076

63   Portrait of Fernande Olivier, 1906
Charcoal, 612 x 458 mm. Zervos VI, no. 747
Gift of Herman Waldeck. 51.210

64   Peasant Girls from Andorra, 1906
Pen and ink, 631 x 431 mm. Zervos VI, no. 780
Gift of Robert Allerton. 30.933

65   Peasant Woman with a Shawl, 1906
Charcoal, 620 x 404 mm
Lent by the Heirs of Pauline Kohlsaat Palmer

66   Two Nudes, 1906
Stumped pencil, 630 x 469 mm
Gift of Mrs. Potter Palmer. 44.575

67   Man with Crossed Hands, 1907
Gouache, 622 x 470 mm. Zervos II, part 1, no. 15
Lent from the Collection of Mr. and Mrs. James W. Alsdorf

68   Still Life, 1907-08
Pen, charcoal, and water color, 337 x 512 mm
Gift of William Eisendrath, Jr. 40.1047

69   Head of a Woman, 1908
Brown wash, 630 x 489 mm. Zervos VI, no. 1120
Lent by Mr. and Mrs. Edwin E. Hokin

70   Head of a Woman, 1909
Black crayon and gouache, 618 x 478 mm
Zervos II, part 1, no. 140
The Charles L. Hutchinson Memorial. 45.136

71   Head, 1909
Brush, ink, and water color, 333 x 255 mm
The Alfred Stieglitz Collection. 49.578

72   Head of a Woman, 1909
Water color and gouache, 310 x 230 mm
Gift of Mr. and Mrs. Roy J. Friedman. 64.215

73   Still Life, 1911
Pen and ink, 325 x 346 mm. Zervos II, part 1, no. 297
Lent by Mr. and Mrs. Michael Braude

74   Still Life with a Bottle, 1912-13
Charcoal and newspaper collage, 605 x 458 mm
Lent by Mr. and Mrs. Morton G. Neumann

75   Still Life with Calling Card, 1914
Crayon and pasted papers, 138 x 208 mm
Zervos II, part 2, no. 490
Lent by Mrs. Gilbert W. Chapman

76   Woman in an Armchair, 1916
Gouache and water color, 153 x 124 mm
Zervos II, part 2, no. 561
Gift of Robert Allerton. 27.545

77   Costume Design for *Pulcinella,* 1917
Gouache, 290 x 216 mm. Zervos III, no. 22
Lent by Mr. and Mrs. Morton G. Neumann

78   Portrait of Massine, 1917
Pencil, 168 x 115 mm
Inscribed: *A Massine/dans le train/pour Naples/Picasso 1917*
and with dedication by Massine: *To charming Bobsy-with my
gratitude-/souvenir of my collection and our/season in Chicago/.
from Leonide/Chicago* [December 1936]
Zervos VI, no. 1341
Gift of Mrs. Gilbert W. Chapman in memory of Charles B.
Goodspeed. 47.874

79   Pierrot and Harlequin, 1918
Pencil, 260 x 216 mm. Zervos II, no. 135
Gift of Mrs. Gilbert W. Chapman in memory of Charles B. Good-
speed. 47.875

80   Pierrot and Harlequin, 1919
Gouache, 257 x 197 mm
Lent by Mrs. Gilbert W. Chapman

81   Nessus and Dejanira
Dated September 14, 1920. Silverpoint, 250 x 324 mm
Zervos VI, no. 1402
Lent by Mr. and Mrs. Morton G. Neumann

82   Nessus and Dejanira
Dated September 22, 1920. Silverpoint on grounded paper,

*Except for those indicated as lent, drawings and prints are from the
collection of The Art Institute of Chicago. In every case, the last line
of the catalogue entry lists the lender, donor, or special collection.*

213 x 270 mm. Zervos VI, no. 1395
The Clarence Buckingham Collection. 65.783

83 Classical Head, ca. 1921
    Colored chalks, 597 x 445 mm
    Lent by The Arts Club of Chicago

84 Young Girl Seated
    Dated March 15, 1921. Pencil, 260 x 204 mm
    Zervos VI, no. 1393
    Lent from the Collection of Mr. and Mrs. James W. Alsdorf

85 Sheet of Figure Studies, ca. 1921-23
    Pen and ink, 228 x 260 mm
    Lent by Mr. and Mrs. Morton G. Neumann

86 Nude, 1923
    Brush and ink, 615 x 470 mm. Zervos V, no. 133
    Lent from the Collection of Mr. and Mrs. James W. Alsdorf

87 The Pipes of Pan, 1923
    Charcoal, 640 x 490 mm
    Bequest of Joseph Winterbotham. 54.336

88 Two Dancers, 1925
    Pen and ink, 350 x 250 mm. Zervos V, no. 430
    Lent by the Heirs of Pauline Kohlsaat Palmer

89 The Flute Player, Dated October 22, 1932
    Pen and ink, 260 x 330 mm. Zervos VIII, no. 45
    Lent by Mr. and Mrs. Joseph R. Shapiro

90 Minotaur and Woman, Dated June 24, 1933
    Pen and black wash on blue paper, 480 x 628 mm
    Zervos VIII, no. 112
    Gift of Margaret Blake. 67.516

91 Minotaur and Wounded Horse, Dated April 17, 1935
    Pen, ink, and crayon, 337 x 537 mm
    Lent anonymously

92 Portrait of Dora Maar, Dated November 6, 1936
    Pencil and crayon, 394 x 304 mm. Zervos VIII, no. 299
    Lent from the Collection of Mr. and Mrs. James W. Alsdorf

93 Woman Seated in a Wicker Chair (Dora Maar)
    Dated May 31, 1938. Pen and ink, 458 x 242 mm
    Lent by Mr. and Mrs. Morton G. Neumann

94 Seated Woman, Dated November 28, 1941
    Gouache, 408 x 305 mm. Zervos XI, no. 353
    Lent by Mr. and Mrs. Joseph R. Shapiro

95 Head of a Young Boy, 1944
    Gouache, 285 x 225 mm. Zervos XIV, no. 31
    Lent by Florene M. Schoenborn

96 Woman Bathing Her Foot, Dated May 6, 1944
    Pencil, 505 x 383 mm. Zervos XIII, no. 291
    Bequest of Curt Valentin. 55.603

97 Seated Woman, Dated December 6, 1953
    Wash, 655 x 504 mm
    Lent by Dr. Paul Sternberg Trusts

98 Studio Scene, Dated December 24, 1953
    Brush and ink, 350 x 268 mm. Zervos XVI, no. 76
    Lent by Mr. and Mrs. Morton G. Neumann

99 In the Studio, Dated January 6, 1954
    Brush and ink, 240 x 320 mm. Zervos XVI, no. 154
    Lent by Mr. and Mrs. Morton G. Neumann

100 The Reading, Dated December 26, 1953
     Pen and brush, 260 x 218 mm. Zervos XVI, no. 93
     Lent by Mr. and Mrs. Edwin E. Hokin

101 Sheet with Six Studies for the Chicago Sculpture, 1962
     Pencil, 415 x 260 mm
     Gift of William E. Hartmann

102 Study for the Chicago Sculpture
     White chalk on plywood, 1000 x 810 mm
     Gift of Pablo Picasso

103 Reclining Woman, Dated January 12, 1964
     Charcoal, 615 x 750 mm
     Lent by Mrs. Samuel E. Johnson

104 Study for the Chicago Sculpture
     Dated April 30, 1965. Pencil, 500 x 113 mm
     Lent by William E. Hartmann

105 Head, Dated July 15, 1965, inscribed "Pour Bill"
     Felt-tipped pen with black ink and red, yellow,
     and blue vegetable pigments, 265 x 210 mm
     Lent by William E. Hartmann

106 Man and Flute Player (recto)
     Dated January 12, 1967
     Colored crayon

106a The Picture Lovers (verso)
      Dated January 12, 1967
      Pen and ink, 503 x 658 mm
      Bequest of Loula Lasker

Prints

107 The Frugal Repast, 1904
Etching printed in blue, 460 x 380 mm. G.2 IIa (first edition)
The Clarence Buckingham Collection. 63.825

108 The Frugal Repast, 1904
Etching printed in black, 460 x 380 mm. G.2 IIa (first edition)
The Alfred Stieglitz Collection. 49.904

109 Two Saltimbanques, 1905
Drypoint, 120 x 9 mm. G.6b (second edition)
The Albert Roullier Memorial Collection. 27.1378

110 Head of a Woman in Profile, 1905
Drypoint, 291 x 250 mm. G.7b (second edition)
Gift of Walter S. Brewster. 48.325

111 Au Cirque, 1905
Drypoint, 220 x 140 mm. G.11b (second edition)
Gift of Walter S. Brewster. 51.326

112 La toilette de la mère, 1905
Drypoint, 235 x 176 mm. G.15b (second edition)
Gift of Mrs. Gilbert W. Chapman in memory of Charles B.
Goodspeed. 47.868

113 Salomé, 1905
Drypoint, 400 x 348 mm. G.17b (second edition)
The Albert H. Wolf Collection. 33.55

114 Bust of a Young Woman, 1906
Woodcut printed in 1933, 557 x 385 mm. G.212
Gift of The Print and Drawing Club. 51.197

115 Still Life with Bottle (Vie Marc), 1912
Drypoint, 500 x 305 mm. G.33b
The John H. Wrenn Memorial Collection. 57.353

116 Portrait of Paul Valéry, 1920
Lithograph, 96 x 88 mm. G.224
Gift of Mrs. Gilbert W. Chapman in memory of Charles B.
Goodspeed. 47.843

117 Reclining Woman, 1924
Lithograph, 216 x 300 mm. G.238
Gift of Walter S. Brewster. 51.331

118 The Studio, 1927
Etching, 350 x 398 mm. G.121
Gift of The Print and Drawing Club. 47.20

119 The Painter and the Model who Knits, 1927
Balzac, Le Chef d'Oeuvre Inconnu, plate 4
Etching, 280 x 194 mm. G.126
Print and Drawing Purchase Fund. 46.440

120 The Artist Before his Painting, 1927
Balzac, Le Chef d'Oeuvre Inconnu, plate 10
Etching, 278 x 194 mm. G.133
Print and Drawing Purchase Fund. 46.440

121 Deucalion and Pyrrha Creating a New Human Species, 1927
Ovid, Metamorphoses, Book 1
Etching, 312 x 224 mm. G.144
Given in memory of A. Peter Dewey. 46.65

122 Visage, 1928
Lithograph, 204 x 142 mm. G.243
Gift of Walter S. Brewster. 52.1189

123 The Loves of Jupiter and Semele, 1930
Ovid, Metamorphoses, Book 3
Etching, 310 x 193 mm. G.148
Given in memory of A. Peter Dewey. 46.65

124 Part of the Female Body, 1931
Ovid, Metamorphoses, Book 14
Etching, 381 x 299 mm. G.169
Given in memory of A. Peter Dewey. 46.65

125 Satyr and Sleeping Woman, 1933
Etching and aquatint, 315 x 417 mm. B.27
Lent by Dr. Eugene A. Solow

126 Embrace, 1933
Etching and drypoint, 197 x 275 mm. B.29
Print and Drawing Purchase Account

127 Embrace, 1933
Etching and aquatint, 196 x 274 mm. B.32
Lent by Dr. Eugene A. Solow

128 The Embrace, 1933
Drypoint, 295 x 365 mm. B.31
Anonymous gift. 63.546

129 Minotaur, Drinking Sculptor, and Three Models, 1933
Etching and drypoint, 297 x 367 mm. B.92
Lent by Mr. and Mrs. Everett Kovler

130 Minotaur and Sleeping Girl, 1933
Drypoint, 295 x 365 mm. B.93
Gift of The Print and Drawing Club. 57.331

131 Minotaur Caressing a Girl, 1933
Etching and drypoint, 297 x 367 mm. B.84
Lent by Mr. and Mrs. Everett Kovler

132 Drinking Minotaur and Sculptor with Two Models, 1933
Etching and drypoint, 295 x 363 mm. B.84
Lent by Dr. Eugene A. Solow

133 Sculptor and Model by a Window, 1933
Etching, 367 x 297 mm. B.68
Lent by Mr. and Mrs. Everett Kovler

134 Four Models and a Sculptured Head, 1933
Etching and drypoint, 231 x 318 mm. B.82
Lent by Dr. Eugene A. Solow

135 Head in Profile, 1933
Aquatint and etching, 177 x 154 mm.
Lent by Mr. and Mrs. Everett Kovler

136 Two Catalan Men, 1933
Etching, printed on parchment, 232 x 287 mm. B.12
Print and Drawing Purchase Fund. 65.788

137 Three Costumed Figures before a Sculptured Bust, 1934 (?)
Etching, printed on parchment, 272 x 178 mm. B.77
The William McCallin McKee Memorial Collection. 46.438

138 Dying Minotaur, 1933
Etching and drypoint, 191 x 265 mm. B.88
Print and Drawing Purchase Fund. 67.532

139 Sculptor and a Statue of Three Female Dancers, 1934
Etching and drypoint, 222 x 313 mm. B.81
Lent by Mr. and Mrs. Everett Kovler

140 Tauromachia, 6/12/34
Etching, 493 x 691 mm.
Bequest of Curt Valentin. 55.623

141 Tauromachia, 9/8/34
Etching, 495 x 689 mm.
Bequest of Curt Valentin. 55.624

142 Minotauromachia, 1935
Etching, 492 x 690 mm.
Inscribed "B.áT." [Bon á tirer]
Gift of Mrs. P. Donnelley. 47.160

143 Blind Minotaur Led through the Night, ca. 1935
Aquatint, 247 x 347 mm. B.97
Lent by Dr. Eugene A. Solow

144 Boy Watching a Sleeping Woman by Candlelight, ca. 1935
Etching and aquatint, 237 x 297 mm. B.26
Lent by Mr. and Mrs. Everett Kovler

145 Four Children Looking at a Monster, ca. 1935
Drypoint, 237 x 297 mm. B.13
Gift of Mr. and Mrs. Samuel E. Johnson

146 Frontispiece to Paul Eluard's La Barre d'Appui, 1936
Etching, 316 x 207 mm.
Lent by Mr. and Mrs. Morton G. Neumann

147 The Combat, 1937
Drypoint, 397 x 493 mm.
Gift of The Print and Drawing Club. 46.49

148 Portrait of Vollard I, 1937
Lift ground etching, 350 x 247 mm. B.98
Print and Drawing Purchase Fund. 55.1113

149 The Tambourine Player, 1938
Aquatint, 665 x 510 mm.
Print and Drawing Purchase Fund. 61.32

Buffon, Histoire Naturelle, 1942
Lift ground etchings
Print and Drawing Purchase Fund. 46.439

150 Donkey, plate 2

151 Bull, plate 4

152 Ostrich, plate 16

153 Turkey, plate 19

154 Frogs in a Pond, plate 26

155 Spider, plate 30

156 The Flea, discarded plate from Buffon, Histoire Naturelle, 1942
Lift ground etching, 370 x 275 mm
Gift of The Print and Drawing Club. 54.17

157 Corrida, 1946
Lithograph, 295 x 430 mm. M.26
Gift of Joseph R. Shapiro. 55.558

158 Centaur and Bacchante, 1947
Lithograph, 490 x 640 mm. M.63
Bequest of Curt Valentin. 55.614

159 Composition with a Vase of Flowers, 1947
Lithograph in three colors, 450 x 600 mm. M.74
Bequest of Curt Valentin. 55.617

160 La Dormeuse, 1947
Lithograph, 500 x 650 mm. M.81
Gift of Mr. and Mrs. Derald H. Ruttenberg. 65.31

161 Femme assise et dormeuse, 1947
Lithograph, 490 x 600 mm. M.104
Gift of The Print and Drawing Club. 49.23

162 David and Bathsheba (after Cranach the Elder), 1948
Lithograph, 760 x 560 mm. M.109bis
Lent by Mr. and Mrs. Morton G. Neumann

163 The Studio, 1948
Lithograph, 610 x 480 mm. M.125
Bequest of Curt Valentin. 55.616

164 Woman in an Armchair No. 1, 1948
Lithograph, 696 x 547 mm. M.134, 3rd state
Bequest of Curt Valentin. 55.617

165 The Dove, 1949
Lithograph, 545 x 700 mm. M.141
Gift of The Print and Drawing Club. 50.27

166 The Lobster, 1949
Lithograph, 546 x 697 mm. M.143
Bequest of Curt Valentin. 55.618

167 The Toad, 1949
Lithograph, 492 x 639 mm. M.144
Lent by Mr. and Mrs. Morton G. Neumann

168 Bust in Modern Style, 1949
Lithograph, 650 x 500 mm. M.164
Bequest of Curt Valentin. 55.619

169 Young Girl Inspired by Cranach the Elder, 1949
Lithograph, 650 x 500 mm. M.176
Gift of Mr. and Mrs. Joseph R. Shapiro. 55.562

170 Figure in a Striped Blouse, 1949
Lithograph in six colors, 652 x 500 mm. M.179
Gift of Mr. and Mrs. Morton G. Neumann. 51.368

171 The Knight and His Page, 1951
Color lithograph, 560 x 660 mm. M.200, final state
Lent by Mr. and Mrs. Morton G. Neumann

172 Paloma with Her Doll, 1952
Lithograph, 550 x 70 mm.
Lent by Mr. and Mrs. Morton G. Neumann

173 The Wounded Picador, 1952
Lift ground etching, 517 x 667 mm.
Gift of Mr. and Mrs. Morton G. Neumann. 53.360

174 Woman at a Window, 1952
Etching and aquatint, 545 x 407 mm.
Lent by Mr. and Mrs. Morton G. Neumann

175 Portrait of a Woman, 1953
Etching and aquatint, 834 x 473 mm.
Bequest of Curt Valentin. 55.613

176 The Rehearsal, 1954
Lithograph, 495 x 654 mm. M.252
Lent by Mr. and Mrs. Lewis Manilow

177 The Family of the Saltimbanque, 1954
Lithograph, 503 x 642 mm. M.249
Gift of The Print and Drawing Club. 54.119

178 Jacqueline Reading, 1957
Lithograph, 555 x 440 mm. M.309, first state
Lent by Mr. and Mrs. Everett Kovler

179 Woman in a Flowered Blouse, 1958
Lithograph, 630 x 480 m. M.307
Lent by Mr. and Mrs. Morton G. Neumann

180 Young Girl (after Cranach the Elder), 1958
Linoleum cut in six colors, 641 x 532 mm.
Lent by Mr. and Mrs. Morton G. Neumann

181 Jacqueline, 1958
Lithograph, 557 x 440 mm. M.310, 3rd state
Gift of Mr. and Mrs. Leigh B. Block. 65.33

182 Picador and Bull, 1959
Linoleum cut in two colors, 530 x 640 mm.
The Walter S. Brewster Collection. 65.517

183 Still Life under a Lamp, 1962
Linoleum cut in color, 530 x 640 mm.
The Joseph R. Shapiro Collection. 65.37